FRANCE ATLAS ROAD MAP 2025

WHETHER YOURE A SEASONED TRAVELER OR
PLANNING YOUR FIRST ADVENTURE THIS ATLAS
BRINGS THE BEAUTY OF FRANCE TO YOUR
FINGERTIPS

JULIEN NICOLAS

Contents

Pavillon de Vendome
arts and culture gallery

France is more than just a country; it's a world of endless discovery, where every road leads to breathtaking landscapes, vibrant cities, and timeless cultural treasures. Whether you dream of wandering through lavender fields in Provence, sipping fine wine in Bordeaux, or marveling at the architectural splendor of Paris, France offers an unparalleled journey for every traveler.

France as a Traveler's Paradise

Few destinations in the world rival France when it comes to diversity. With its rich tapestry of history, art, and natural wonders, it's no surprise that millions of visitors flock here each year. France offers something for everyone: serene countryside retreats, bustling metropolises, sun-drenched coastlines, and snow-capped Alpine peaks.

Comprehensive Guide for Road Trippers

There's a unique sense of freedom in exploring a country by road. Driving in France unlocks opportunities to wander off the beaten path, stumble upon charming villages, and connect with local culture in ways that no other mode of travel allows. This guide is your ultimate companion for road trips, providing detailed maps, practical advice, and handpicked recommendations for routes that suit every kind of traveler. Whether you're planning a scenic journey along the French Riviera or a historical tour through Normandy, this book ensures you won't miss a thing.

Highlighting France's Unique Treasures

France is a land of contrasts, where history meets modernity and nature blends harmoniously with urban sophistication. This book shines a spotlight on the country's most remarkable features, including.

Geographical wonders like the gorges du verdon and the Pyrenees Mountains.

Historical landmarks such as the Palace of Versailles and the D-Day beaches.

Cultural highlights include the wine regions of Burgundy and Alsace and the culinary delights of Lyon. With this France Atlas Road Map 2025, you'll have the tools to uncover these treasures at your own pace, making every moment of your journey unforgettable.

Road Trip Enthusiasts

If the open road calls your name, this book is your perfect companion. With detailed itineraries and expert driving tips, you'll be equipped to navigate France's diverse landscapes, from its rolling countryside to its rugged coastlines. Each section provides insights into the best routes, scenic detours, and must-see stops, ensuring your road trip is as smooth as it is exhilarating.

First-Time Visitors and Seasoned Travelers

For first-timers, the book serves as a comprehensive introduction to France, answering all your questions about driving, local customs, and essential landmarks. For seasoned travelers, it dives deeper, offering fresh perspectives and lesser-known destinations to reignite your love for this enchanting country.

Historians, Nature Lovers, and Culinary Adventurers

History Buffs: Step back in time as you explore the birthplace of revolutions, the haunting battlefields of World Wars, and the grand châteaux of the Loire Valley.

Nature Enthusiasts: Discover breathtaking natural landscapes, from the snow-dusted peaks of the French Alps to the serene beaches of Corsica. This guide highlights national parks, hiking trails, and other outdoor adventures perfect for nature lovers.

Food and Wine Aficionados: France is synonymous with gastronomy, and this book celebrates the nation's culinary excellence. Follow wine routes through Bordeaux and Champagne, indulge in Parisian pastries, and taste the hearty dishes of rural France.

Connecting with the Reader

Whether you're planning a short getaway or an extended journey, France Atlas Road Map 2025 is more than just a guidebook—it's your trusted travel partner. Its pages are filled with expert insights, heartfelt recommendations, and a passion for helping you experience France in the most authentic and fulfilling way possible.

So buckle up, set your GPS, and prepare to explore the endless beauty and charm of France. Let this book inspire your adventure, answer your questions, and guide you to memories that will last a lifetime.

Welcome to the journey of a lifetime

What Readers Will Learn: Unveiling the Essence of France on the Road

Regional Highlights of France

France is made up of several distinct areas, each with its charm, culture, and landscape. This book delves into every corner of the country, from its bustling urban centers to its tranquil countryside retreats. Readers will learn:

The Distinct Personalities of Each Region

The romantic allure of Paris and Île-de-France is home to iconic landmarks like the Eiffel Tower and the Louvre.

The sun-soaked splendor of Provence and the french Riviera, with its lavender fields, azure coastlines, and glamorous cities like Nice.

Normandy's historical richness is well-known for the famous Mont-Saint-Michel and its D-Day beaches.

The Alpine majesty of the Auvergne-Rhône-Alpes, where mont Blanc reigns supreme.

Unforgettable Must-Sees and Local Secrets

Journey through the vineyards of bordeaux and Burgundy, where some of the world's finest wines are produced.

Experience the wild allure of Corsica, renowned as the "Island of Beauty."

Immerse yourself in the medieval charm of Alsace, with its half-timbered houses and fairytale-like villages.

This book is your gateway to experiencing the true essence of each region, providing a roadmap to the highlights that define France's diverse character.

Navigational Tips for Drivers in France

Driving in a foreign country can be daunting, but with the right guidance, it transforms into an empowering adventure. Here's what readers will gain:

Understanding French Roads

Insights into navigating the country's extensive network of highways (auto routes), rural roads, and scenic byways.

Key differences between toll roads and free roads, including tips for paying tolls efficiently.

Driving Etiquette and Safety Tips

Essential road signs and their meanings, ensuring smooth travel and adherence to local rules.

Advice on handling roundabouts, a staple of French roadways, and understanding priority rules like priorité à droite (priority to the right).

Parking Tips and Solutions

How to decode parking signs, locate available spaces, and avoid hefty fines in both cities and small towns.

The advantages of using parking apps and pre-booking spots for popular destinations.

Updated Driving Laws and Regulations for 2025

France has a dynamic set of driving laws that can evolve year by year, and being informed is essential for a safe journey.

Latest Updates for 2025

Speed limit adjustments on various roads and special regulations in eco-zones.

Introduction of new emissions regulations in major cities, including how to obtain a Crit'Air sticker for your vehicle.

Practical Tips for Foreign Drivers

Required documents and items to carry such as a valid driver's license, vehicle registration, and safety equipment like reflective vests and warning triangles.

Rules for using GPS systems, including avoiding software that identifies speed cameras.

Understanding Fines and Enforcement

How traffic violations are handled for non-residents and how to resolve fines if necessary.

Tips on avoiding common pitfalls like using a mobile phone while driving or neglecting to use headlights in poor weather conditions.

Hidden Gems and Popular Destinations

Beyond the world famous attractions, France is brimming with hidden treasures that make every trip unforgettable. This book ensures you'll experience:

Hidden Gems

Lesser-known villages like Collonges-la-Rouge with its striking red sandstone architecture or Eguisheim, a picturesque village nestled in Alsace's vineyards.

Remote natural wonders such as Camargue's wetlands, teeming with wildlife, or the dramatic cliffs of Étretat in Normandy.

Popular Destinations, Reimagined

Fresh perspectives on iconic landmarks like the Eiffel Tower, Versailles, and Louvre Museum, ensuring you make the most of your visit.

Unique approaches to explore busy hotspots, such as early morning visits, guided tours, or alternative viewing points.

Why This Matters to You

By the end of this book, you won't just know where to go and how to get there—you'll have the confidence and insight to create a journey uniquely your own. With this guide in hand, you'll experience France not just as a tourist, but as an explorer, uncovering its soul one region, road, and hidden gem at a time.

Get ready to navigate France with ease, confidence, and a spirit of adventure. Your unforgettable journey awaits!

SCAN HERE

HOW TO USE QR CODE

- Open your phone's camera app or download scanner app from play store or apple store
- Point the camera at the QR code for a few seconds (no need to take a photo).
- A link should appear on the display, leading you to the location of the code

Chapter 1

Navigating France a Traveler's Guide

Overview of France's Road Network

France boasts one of the most extensive and well-maintained road networks in Europe, making it a dream destination for road trippers. With over a million kilometers of paved roads connecting bustling cities, quaint villages, and breathtaking natural wonders, navigating the French countryside or cityscapes is as much a part of the adventure as reaching your destination. Whether you're planning to explore the scenic coastline of the French Riviera or meander through the wine regions of Bordeaux and Burgundy, understanding the types of roads, toll systems, and road signs is essential for a smooth journey.

Types of Roads

France's road network is divided into several categories, each designed to serve specific types of travel. Here's what you need to know about the major road types

Autoroutes (Motorways)

Purpose: The autoroutes are France's equivalent of highways, designed for long-distance, high-speed travel.

Key Features

Marked with an "A" followed by a number (e.g., A6, A13).

The usual speed restrictions are 110 km/h (68 mph) in rainy weather and 130 km/h (80 mph) in dry weather, though they can vary.

Equipped with service areas (aires), offering fuel, restrooms, and sometimes restaurants or picnic areas.

Tolls: Most autoroutes are toll roads, and the fees are based on distance traveled.

Routes Nationales (National Roads)

Purpose: Managed by the government, these roads connect major cities and regions without the toll costs associated with autoroutes.

Key Features

Identified by an "N" followed by a number (e.g. N7 or N20).

Depending on the location, speed restrictions often fall between 90 km/h (56 mph) and 110 km/h (68 mph).

Routes nationales often pass through smaller towns, offering a more scenic, albeit slower, and alternative to autoroutes.

Routes Départementales (Departmental Roads)

Purpose: These roads form the backbone of France's local road network, connecting towns, villages, and rural areas.

Key Features

Marked with a "D" followed by a number (e.g., D35, D914).

Speed limits vary from 50 km/h (31 mph) in villages to 80-90 km/h (50-56 mph) on rural roads.

Ideal for exploring off-the-beaten-path destinations and immersing yourself in local culture.

City and Urban Roads

Found within towns and cities, these roads are often busy and include roundabouts, pedestrian crossings, and designated cycling lanes.

Speed limits are typically 50 km/h (31 mph) unless otherwise posted, with 30 km/h (18 mph) zones in residential areas or near schools.

Tolls and Their Payment Systems

If you plan to use the autoroutes, it's essential to familiarize yourself with the toll system (péages), which is straightforward but different from many other countries

How Tolls Work

Toll booths are located at the entrance and/or exit of autoroutes.

You take a ticket upon entering the toll road and pay the fee based on the distance traveled when exiting.

Payment Methods

Cash: Most toll booths accept cash payments. Ensure you have smaller denominations and coins for convenience.

Credit/Debit Cards: Most major cards are accepted, but having a chip-and-PIN card is advisable.

Electronic Toll Tags: For frequent travelers, a Télépéage badge offers a convenient option, allowing you to drive through tolls without stopping.

Toll Costs

Toll charges vary depending on the distance, vehicle type, and specific autoroute. Expect to pay approximately €10-15 per 100 kilometers for a standard car.

Tips for Using Tolls

Look for the correct lane

Green Arrows: Open for cash and card payments.

"CB" Symbol: Card-only lanes.

Orange "T": Reserved for Télépéage users.

Keep your ticket safe, as losing it may result in being charged the maximum toll fee.

Tips for Understanding French Road Signs

French road signs follow international conventions but have a few unique features worth noting. Mastering these signs is crucial for navigating safely and confidently.

Directional Signs

Blue Signs: Indicate autoroutes (motorways).

Green Signs: Used for routes nationales and major roads.

White Signs: Direct to smaller towns and local destinations.

Speed Limit Signs

Speed limits are displayed within a red-bordered circle, often accompanied by weather-based variations:

Dry conditions: 130 km/h on autoroutes, 90 km/h on national roads, and 50 km/h in cities.

Wet conditions or for novice drivers: Reduced limits apply.

Priority and Yield Signs

Yellow Diamond: Indicates a road with priority over intersecting roads.

Inverted Triangle (Yield): this indicates that you have to give way to oncoming traffic.

Stop Sign: Marked in French as "STOP" (easy for English speakers to recognize).

Warning Signs

Triangular with a red border, these signs alert drivers to potential hazards like sharp bends, wildlife crossings, or steep gradients.

Unique Signs in France

Priorité à Droite: This rule means you must yield to vehicles coming from your right at unmarked intersections.

Environmental Zones: In low-emission zones (e.g., Paris), special signs require drivers to display a Crit'Air sticker indicating their vehicle's emission class.

Key Takeaways

Navigating France by road is a rewarding experience that blends the thrill of exploration with the practicality of convenience.

Essential Tools for Navigation

Navigating the vast and varied landscape of France can be a seamless experience when equipped with the right tools. Whether you're exploring bustling cities, meandering through quaint villages, or venturing into the countryside, effective navigation is the key to enjoying your journey without unnecessary detours or stress. These are Navigation options for road trips across France, helping you choose the tools that fit your travel style and needs.

GPS Systems and Their Reliability in France

Global Positioning Systems (GPS) are among the most reliable and user-friendly tools for navigation in France. Modern GPS devices and apps have revolutionized travel, offering real-time directions, traffic updates, and alternative routes.

Advantages of GPS in France

Real-Time Updates

GPS systems like Garmin, TomTom, and vehicle-integrated systems provide live traffic data, helping avoid congested areas or roadblocks.

Some GPS devices even alert drivers to roadwork, accidents, or temporary detours.

Accuracy and Coverage

GPS is highly accurate in France, covering everything from major autoroutes to rural departmental roads.

Satellite coverage ensures you won't lose your way, even in remote areas like the Massif Central or the Alsace wine route.

Customizable Features

Many systems allow you to set preferences for avoiding toll roads, favoring scenic routes, or calculating the fastest paths.

Language options make these tools accessible to non-French speakers.

Challenges with GPS

Signal Issues: In very remote or mountainous regions, such as the Alps or Pyrenees, GPS signals can occasionally falter.

Over-Reliance: Blindly trusting GPS can lead to missed opportunities to explore unmarked scenic routes or hidden gems.

Tips for Using GPS in France

Ensure your GPS maps are updated before your trip to include new roads or traffic patterns.

Pair your GPS with a backup tool, such as a map or app, to cover potential signal outages.

Popular Travel Apps for Mapping and Points of Interest

Smartphone travel apps have become indispensable companions for road trippers. In addition to offering navigation, many apps also provide information on points of interest, accommodations, dining options, and fuel stations.

Best Travel Apps for France

Google Maps

Features: Turn-by-turn directions, live traffic updates, walking and cycling routes.

Unique Perks: Extensive coverage of local businesses, including reviews and hours of operation.

Drawbacks: Consumes significant mobile data if offline maps are not downloaded in advance.

Waze

Features: Crowdsourced traffic information, including speed traps, accidents, and road closures.

Unique Perks: Real-time community alerts make it excellent for navigating busy urban areas like Paris or Lyon.

Drawbacks: May not be as effective in rural regions where fewer users contribute data.

Park4Night

Features: Identifies parking areas, campgrounds, and overnight stops.

Unique Perks: Tailored for road trippers with campervans or RVs.

Drawbacks: Limited usefulness for those traveling by car and staying in hotels.

Maps.me

Features: Offline maps, making it a great backup option for areas with poor connectivity.

Unique Perks: Lightweight and easy to use.

Drawbacks: Lacks the robust real-time features of Google Maps or Waze.

Tips for Using Travel Apps

Download offline maps of your planned destinations in case of limited network access.

Use apps to discover nearby attractions, such as historic sites, local eateries, and scenic viewpoints.

Traditional Paper Maps and Why They Still Matter

In an age of digital navigation, paper maps might seem outdated, but they remain a valuable tool for travelers in France. For certain scenarios, they provide unmatched reliability and an enjoyable tactile experience.

Advantages of Paper Maps

Paper maps don't require batteries, internet access, or GPS signals, making them a fail-safe option in remote areas or during power outages.

Big-Picture Perspective

Unlike digital maps, paper maps offer a broad overview of the region, helping you plan routes and identify nearby points of interest at a glance.

Cultural Experience

Studying and using a map can enrich your journey, fostering a deeper connection to the geography and history of the region.

Best Paper Maps for France

Michelin Maps: Renowned for their accuracy and detail, Michelin maps are categorized by region and include scenic routes, toll roads, and points of interest.

Learning Curve: For those unfamiliar with reading maps, navigation might feel slower or more challenging.

Tips for Using Paper Map

Pair your map with a compass for enhanced orientation.

Highlight your planned route and mark stops to make navigation easier.

Keep the map in a waterproof or protective cover to prevent damage.

Finding the Perfect Navigation Combo

To make the most of your French road trip, consider combining multiple navigation tools. For example

Use a GPS or app like Google Maps for real-time navigation.

Carry a paper map as a backup for rural or mountainous areas.

Leverage apps like ViaMichelin to estimate tolls and fuel costs during route planning.

By blending technology with tried-and-true methods, you'll be prepared for any navigation challenge, ensuring a smoother and more enjoyable journey.

Driving in France offers an unparalleled opportunity to explore its rich tapestry of landscapes, from the rugged cliffs of Normandy to the sun-drenched fields of Provence. However, ensuring a safe journey requires understanding road safety protocols and being prepared for potential challenges. In this section, we'll cover essential road safety tips, including emergency resources, common driving hazards, and proactive measures for a smooth and secure trip.

Emergency Numbers and Roadside Assistance Services

Being prepared for emergencies is crucial, whether you're driving in bustling urban centers or remote rural areas. France has an efficient network of emergency services and roadside assistance programs to aid travelers.

Key Emergency Numbers in France

112: The universal emergency number for all EU countries, including France. It can be dialed for police, fire, or medical assistance in emergencies.

15: Direct number for medical emergencies (SAMU).

17: Police emergency line.

18: Fire services.

Roadside Assistance Services

Autoroute Emergency Phones

Along French motorways (autoroutes), you'll find orange emergency phones approximately every two kilometers. These connect directly to local road assistance services.

Use these instead of your mobile phone when possible, as they provide your precise location automatically.

Major Roadside Assistance Providers

Vinci Autoroutes: Operates services on many toll roads; their helpline is available in English at +33 800 100 200.

AXA Assistance: Offers support for travelers who have breakdown coverage with their insurance.

Automobile Club Association (ACA): Similar to AAA in the U.S., they offer a range of assistance services for members.

Tips for Managing Emergencies on the Road

Carry a European accident report form (constat amiable d'accident) to simplify reporting incidents.

Keep a basic roadside emergency kit in your car, including a reflective vest, warning triangle (both mandatory in France), flashlight, and first-aid supplies.

Common Driving Hazards in France

While France is generally a safe place to drive, understanding the country's unique road conditions can help you avoid potential pitfalls.

Weather-Related Hazards

France's varied geography results in diverse weather patterns, which can pose challenges for drivers.

Rain and Slippery Roads:

In regions like Brittany or Normandy, sudden rain showers can create slick road surfaces, especially on older pavements.

Reduce speed and increase the following distance during wet conditions.

Snow and Ice

In winter, mountainous areas such as the Alps and Pyrenees experience heavy snowfall. Snow chains or winter tires may be mandatory in these regions.

Check weather forecasts and road conditions before traveling.

Fog

Common in valleys and near bodies of water, especially in autumn.

Turn on low-beam headlights or fog lights to enhance visibility.

Rural Roads and Countryside Challenges

Exploring France's charming rural roads offers stunning scenery but also unique hazards:

Narrow and Winding Roads

Many rural roads, especially in older villages, are narrow and lack clear markings. Be sure to drive carefully and be ready to yield to traffic.

Farm Vehicles

In agricultural regions like Dordogne or Burgundy, you may encounter slow-moving tractors. Be patient and only overtake when it's safe and permitted.

Wildlife Crossings

In forested areas, such as the Ardennes or the Vosges, animals like deer can cross roads unexpectedly, especially at dawn or dusk.

City-Specific Hazards

Driving in French cities comes with its own set of challenges:

Congestion

Cities like paris, lyon, and marseille often experience heavy traffic, particularly during rush hours. Plan routes carefully and consider parking on the outskirts while using public transport.

Scooters and Bicycles

Cyclists and scooter riders frequently share the road, particularly in urban areas. Always check blind spots before turning or opening doors.

Roundabouts

France has over 30,000 roundabouts, many of which require yielding to traffic already inside the circle. Learn the rules to navigate them confidently.

Additional Tips for Staying Safe

Understand French Driving Laws

Keep your driver's license, vehicle registration, and insurance documents with you at all times.

Make sure your vehicle is equipped with the required items, such as a reflective vest and a warning triangle.

Stay Alert

Take breaks every two hours to combat fatigue, especially on long drives. French autoroutes have rest areas (aires) that often include picnic spots and fuel stations.

Watch for Speed Cameras

France enforces strict speed limits with the widespread use of automated cameras. Fines can be steep and are often mailed to international drivers.

Avoid Driving Under the Influence

France's legal blood alcohol limit is 0.05%, lower than in many countries. For bus drivers or new drivers, the limit is even stricter at 0.02%.

Use public transport or taxis if you plan to drink, especially in wine regions.

Child Safety

Children under 10 years old must sit in the back seat unless the vehicle lacks rear seats.

Young children are required to use approved car seats or booster seats.

Night Driving

While roads are generally well-lit in cities, rural roads can be dark and less maintained. Use high beams carefully to prevent dazzling oncoming drivers.

Proactive Preparation for a Safe Journey

Plan your routes and familiarize yourself with alternative roads.

Download weather and traffic apps for real-time updates.

Inform someone of your travel plans, especially if heading to remote areas.

By staying prepared, understanding local driving conditions, and following these safety tips, you can focus on enjoying France's breathtaking landscapes and rich cultural offerings without worry.

Chapter 2

Regional Highlights of France

France is a country of remarkable diversity, where each region boasts its unique blend of history, culture, and landscapes. From the windswept coastlines of Normandy to the bustling streets of Paris, Northern France encapsulates this variety. This is the highlights of Normandy, Hauts-de-France, and Paris with Île-de-France, offering insights into their iconic landmarks, cultural heritage, and practical tips for travelers.

Northern France

Northern France, characterized by its dramatic coastlines, lush countryside, and poignant history, is a must-visit region for anyone seeking a rich cultural and historical experience.

Normandy: A Tapestry of History and Beauty

Normandy is synonymous with its World War II history, but its appeal extends far beyond its war stories. This region offers a mix of natural beauty, architectural wonders, and quaint villages.

1. The D-day Beaches

Historical Significance

The beaches of Normandy—Omaha, Utah, Gold, Juno, and Sword—were the sites of the D-Day landings during World War II. These significant events signaled the start of Western Europe's liberation.

Must-Visit Spots:

Omaha Beach: Known for its harrowing stories of heroism, this beach also features the Normandy American Cemetery and Memorial.

Arromanches: Explore the remnants of the Mulberry Harbor, a logistical marvel of the war.

2. Mont Saint-Michel

Architectural Marvel:

Rising majestically from a tidal island, Mont Saint-Michel is an iconic abbey that has drawn pilgrims for centuries. Its Gothic spires, winding streets, and panoramic views make it a must-see.

Practical Tips

Before you go, check the tide schedules to make the most of its special location.

Take the shuttle bus to the entrance after parking in the approved spots.

3. Picturesque Villages

Normandy is dotted with charming villages that exude rustic beauty

Honfleur: A harbor town that inspired artists likes Monet, known for its timber-framed houses and vibrant art scene.

Hauts-de-France: Rich History and Modern Charm

Hauts-de-France, located in the northernmost part of the country, is steeped in history yet brimming with modern vitality.

1. Lille: A Cultural Hub

Architectural Highlights

Lille is renowned for its Flemish-inspired architecture. The Grand Place is a stunning square framed by vibrant facades, including the historic Old Stock Exchange (Vieille Bourse).

Cultural Attractions:

Palais des Beaux-Arts: France's second-largest art museum, featuring works by Rubens, Van Dyck, and Delacroix.

La Piscine Museum: A former Art Deco swimming pool turned museum in nearby Roubaix.

2. Somme Battlefields

Historical Significance

The Somme region was the site of one of World War I's bloodiest battles. It is a touching reminder of the sacrifices made during the Great War today.

Key Sites to Visit

Thiepval Memorial: Honoring the missing soldiers from Britain and South Africa.

Beaumont-Hamel Newfoundland Memorial: A preserved battlefield offering a glimpse into the harsh realities of trench warfare.

Driving Tips for Northern France

Many rural roads in this region are narrow and bordered by hedgerows, so drive cautiously, especially at night.

Pay attention to seasonal weather, as fog and rain can create challenging driving conditions.

Iconic Landmarks in Paris

1. The Eiffel Tower

No journey to France is truly complete without marveling at the iconic Eiffel Tower.

Best Viewing Tips: For a unique perspective, consider visiting at night when the tower sparkles every hour.

To steer clear of crowds, purchase tickets online ahead of time or enjoy a picnic with a view from the Champ de Mars.

2. The Louvre Museum

Art and History

The Louvre, housing the Mona Lisa and numerous other masterpieces, is a rich repository of art and history.

Navigating the Museum: Focus on one or two sections per visit to avoid being overwhelmed. Use the museum's app for a guided experience.

3. Versailles Palace

Opulent Grandeur

Located just outside Paris, the Palace of Versailles dazzles with its Hall of Mirrors, sprawling gardens, and rich royal history.

Tips for Touring: Visit early to avoid the afternoon crowds. Don't miss the Petit Trianon and Marie Antoinette's estate for a more intimate experience.

Driving Tips for Paris and Surroundings

Driving in Paris is not for the faint-hearted, but with careful planning, it can be manageable.

1. Understanding Traffic Patterns

Parisian streets often feature roundabouts, one-way roads, and narrow lanes. For guidance, use a trustworthy GPS or navigation app.

2. Parking Challenges

Park-and-Ride Options: Avoid driving directly into the city center. Instead, park at designated lots on the outskirts and use public transport to explore.

Île-de-France beyond Paris

The Île-de-France region has so much more to offer beyond the capital

1. Fontainebleau

A stunning royal palace surrounded by a lush forest, perfect for hiking and picnics.

2. Provins

A medieval town known for its well preserved walls, historic fairs, and reenactments of knight tournaments.

From the poignant history of Normandy and the Somme to the grandeur of Paris and the quiet charm of Hauts-de-France, Northern France offers something for every traveler. Regardless of your interests—history, art, or adventure—this area will enthrall you and create lifelong memories. Prepare to immerse yourself in its beauty, and don't forget your camera—it's impossible to resist capturing the magic of these destinations!

Western France

The western region of France is a treasure trove of maritime beauty, medieval history, and wine-soaked adventures. It's perfect for travelers looking to combine coastal tranquility with rich cultural experiences.

Brittany: A Coastal and Cultural Gem

Brittany is celebrated for its dramatic coastline, charming historic towns, and rich Celtic heritage. This northwestern region is a paradise for road-trippers who love dramatic seascapes and charming villages.

1. Coastal Roads and Lighthouses

Must-Drive Routes

The Pink Granite Coast (Côte de Granit Rose) offers breathtaking views of rock formations sculpted by the sea.

The Crozon Peninsula boasts panoramic drives along cliffs, with stops at Cap de la Chèvre and Pointe de Pen-Hir.

Lighthouses

Brittany is dotted with historic lighthouses, such as Phare d'Eckmühl and Phare de Ploumanac'h, offering striking photography opportunities.

2. Medieval Towns

Saint-Malo:

A walled city steeped in maritime history, with cobblestone streets, stunning ocean views, and fresh seafood. Don't pass up the opportunity to stroll along its walls.

Dinan:

A picture-perfect medieval village includes a charming riverbank, small lanes, and half-timbered buildings.

3. Celtic Culture and Traditions

Brittany's festivals celebrate its Celtic heritage

Festival Interceltique de Lorient: A lively gathering of Celtic music, dance, and traditions.

Gastronomic Delights: Indulge in Breton specialties like galettes (savory buckwheat crêpes) and cider.

Loire Valley: Châteaux and Vineyards

The Loire Valley, famously known as the "Garden of France," is celebrated for its breathtaking châteaux, vibrant vineyards, and serene waterways.

1. Iconic Châteaux

Château de Chambord

A Renaissance masterpiece encircled by vast gardens and forests. An architectural wonder is its double-helix staircase.

Château de Chenonceau:

Spanning the Cher River, this château is famed for its elegant architecture and connection to powerful women in French history.

Château d'Azay-le-Rideau:

Nestled on an island, this fairy-tale castle is a perfect blend of charm and grandeur.

2. Wine Country Road Trips

Sancerre and Chinon:

Explore the Loire Valley's famous wine-producing regions, sampling crisp whites and robust reds.

Tasting Tours:

Many vineyards offer guided tastings and tours, providing insights into winemaking traditions.

3. Cycling and Driving Along the Loire River

The Loire à Vélo is a popular cycling route, but drivers can follow scenic paths along the river, stopping at charming villages and markets.

Southern France

The southern regions of France epitomize warmth, beauty, and cultural richness. With Mediterranean coastlines, ancient ruins, and hilltop villages, this area promises an unforgettable journey.

Provence: Where Beauty Meets History

Provence enchants visitors with its lavender fields, Roman heritage, and timeless villages.

1. Lavender Fields

Best viewed in summer, these fields blanket the region with vibrant purple hues and soothing fragrances.

Top Spots

The Valensole Plateau and Sénanque Abbey, where the contrast of lavender and stone architecture is breathtaking.

2. Hilltop Villages

Gordes

Perched on a cliff, this village offers cobbled streets and panoramic views.

Roussillon:

Famous for its ochre cliffs and earthy tones, this village is a painter's dream.

Côte d'Azur: Glamour and Scenic Drives

The French Riviera, or Côte d'Azur, is the epitome of Mediterranean allure, with its glamorous beaches, vibrant cities, and stunning coastal drives.

1. Scenic Coastal Drives

The Corniche Roads between Nice and Monaco offer spectacular views of the sea, cliffs, and luxurious villas.

Stop at Èze, a medieval village perched high above the coastline, for breathtaking vistas.

2. Glamorous Beaches and Cities

Saint-Tropez:

Golden beaches and vibrant nightlife make this place a popular destination for the wealthy and well-known.

Cannes:

Famous for its film festival, this city combines cultural events with pristine beaches.

Occitanie: History and Serenity

Occitanie combines medieval history with tranquil waterways, making it a haven for history buffs and nature enthusiasts.

1. Carcassonne

Fortified City

This UNESCO-listed medieval city boasts towering walls, turrets, and a labyrinth of cobbled streets. A walk along the ramparts offers a step back in time.

2. Canal du Midi

Tranquil Cruises:

The Canal du Midi, another UNESCO World Heritage site, offers serene boat rides through picturesque countryside.

Cycling and Walking Paths:

Trails along the canal are perfect for leisurely exploration of nearby villages and vineyards.

Western and Southern France captures the essence of adventure and discovery. Whether you're drawn to Brittany's Celtic traditions, the Loire Valley's regal châteaux, Provence's aromatic landscapes, or the Côte d'Azur's glamour, these regions promise unforgettable memories for every traveler. Let these highlights inspire your journey through the heart of France.

Eastern France

Eastern France is a blend of contrasting experiences, ranging from the serene wine-producing areas of Alsace and Burgundy to the dramatic peaks of the French Alps. This region is a dream for wine enthusiasts, outdoor adventurers, and cultural explorers.

Alsace: A Symphony of Wine and Architecture

Alsace, located near the German border, is renowned for its picturesque half-timbered villages, world-class wines, and vibrant cultural heritage.

1. The Alsace Wine Route

Overview:

Stretching over 170 kilometers, the Alsace Wine Route is a scenic journey through vineyards and charming towns.

Must-Visit Stops

Riquewihr: Known as one of France's most beautiful villages, this medieval town is surrounded by vineyards.

Eguisheim: Famous for its concentric streets and wine-tasting opportunities.

2. Gastronomic Delights

Pair the region's crisp white wines, like Riesling and Gewürztraminer, with Alsatian dishes such as tarte flambée (a thin-crust pizza) and choucroute garnie (sauerkraut with sausages).

3. Half-Timbered Villages

Walk through villages that seem plucked from a fairy tale, with flower-filled balconies, cobblestone streets, and a backdrop of rolling vineyards.

Burgundy: The Heart of French Wine and Cuisine

Burgundy is synonymous with indulgence, offering a sensory journey through its vineyards, historic towns, and culinary traditions.

1. Legendary Wine Routes

Côte de Nuits and Côte de Beaune:

Renowned for producing some of the finest Pinot Noir and Chardonnay globally, these iconic wine regions are a true delight for connoisseurs.

Numerous vineyards provide wine-making seminars, tours, and tastings.

Beaune

Known as the wine capital of Burgundy, this charming town is home to the Hôtel-Dieu, a stunning medieval hospital turned museum.

2. Gastronomy

Burgundy's cuisine is legendary:

Boeuf Bourguignon: Beef stewed in red wine, a dish that embodies the region's culinary excellence.

Escargots de Bourgogne are snails prepared with herbs, parsley, and garlic butter.

Rhône-Alpes: Mountains and Gastronomy

The Rhône-Alpes region is a paradise for nature enthusiasts and food lovers, blending Alpine majesty with a thriving culinary scene.

1. The French Alps

Winter Sports

Ski resorts like Chamonix and Courchevel are well-known in the French Alps. Summer Adventures:

During the warmer seasons, activities like hiking, mountain biking, and paragliding are widely enjoyed.

Scenic Drives:

Routes like the Route des Grandes Alpes offer stunning views of mountain peaks, valleys, and lakes.

2. Lyon: The Culinary Capital

Food Scene:

Lyon is well-known for its bouchons, which are classic eateries that serve substantial regional fare.

Don't miss quenelles, a fish dumpling in a creamy sauce, and praline tarts.

Cultural Gems: Discover the Renaissance charm of Vieux Lyon and the ancient Roman amphitheater at Fourvière.

Discover the Renaissance charm of Vieux Lyon and the ancient Roman amphitheater at Fourvière.

Central France

The central region of France is often overlooked but offers a unique blend of natural beauty, history, and tranquility.

Auvergne: Land of Volcanoes and Quiet Charm

Auvergne's volcanic landscapes and tranquil villages provide an off-the-beaten-path experience for travelers.

1. Volcanic Landscapes

Parc Naturel Régional des Volcans d'Auvergne:

Home to beautiful hiking paths, verdant meadows, and dormant volcanoes.

Puy de Dôme:

A must-see volcanic peak with panoramic views accessible by a cog railway or a challenging hike.

2. Cheese and Cuisine

Sample local specialties like Saint-Nectaire cheese and truffle, a dish of potatoes and melted cheese.

Limousin: The Hidden Gem of Central France

Limousin, often referred to as France's best-kept secret, offers serene countryside and a rich historical heritage.

1. Peaceful Countryside

Rolling hills, lush meadows, and quiet roads make this region perfect for scenic drives.

Visit Lake Vassivière, a tranquil spot for boating, fishing, and picnics.

2. Historical Gems

Oradour-sur-Glane:

A preserved village destroyed during WWII serves as a poignant reminder of history.

Collonges-la-Rouge:

Known as the "Village of a Thousand Towers," this town is famous for its red sandstone buildings.

3. Artisanal Craftsmanship

Limousin is renowned for its porcelain, particularly in Limoges, where you can tour factories and shop for exquisite pieces.

Overseas France

France's overseas territories add a touch of the exotic, offering road trip opportunities in breathtaking locales.

1. Corsica: The Island of Beauty

Road Travel Tips:

Corsica's winding mountain roads and coastal routes provide dramatic scenery. Drive carefully as some roads can be narrow and steep.

Top Destinations:

Calvi and Bonifacio: Coastal towns with stunning views and rich history.

Scandola Nature Reserve: Accessible by boat, this UNESCO-listed site showcases Corsica's wild beauty.

2. Réunion: A Volcanic Paradise

Driving Adventures:

Discover the island's varied topography, which includes lush woods and volcanic craters.

Routes like the Piton de la Fournaise volcanic drive are unforgettable.

Highlights:

Cilaos and Salazie: Mountain villages nestled in volcanic calderas.

Black Sand Beaches: Found along the island's coast, offering a unique contrast to the lush interior.

Whether traversing the wine routes of Alsace, exploring the volcanic wonders of Auvergne, or navigating Corsica's coastal roads, these regions promise a road trip filled with discovery, culture, and natural beauty. France's regional diversity ensures every traveler finds something to captivate their spirit.

France

SCAN HERE

HOW TO USE QR CODE

- Open your phone's camera app or download scanner app from play store or apple store
- Point the camera at the QR code for a few seconds (no need to take a photo).
- A link should appear on the display, leading you to the location of the code

Normandy

SCAN HERE

HOW TO USE QR CODE

- Open your phone's camera app or download scanner app from play store or apple store
- Point the camera at the QR code for a few seconds (no need to take a photo).
- A link should appear on the display, leading you to the location of the code

Omaha Beach

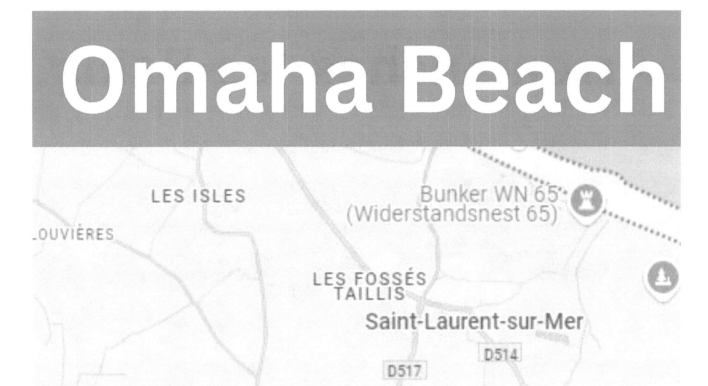

SCAN HERE

HOW TO USE QR CODE

- Open your phone's camera app or download scanner app from play store or apple store
- Point the camera at the QR code for a few seconds (no need to take a photo).
- A link should appear on the display, leading you to the location of the code

Arromanches-les-Bains

SCAN HERE

HOW TO USE QR CODE

- Open your phone's camera app or download scanner app from play store or apple store
- Point the camera at the QR code for a few seconds (no need to take a photo).
- A link should appear on the display, leading you to the location of the code

Mont Saint-Michel

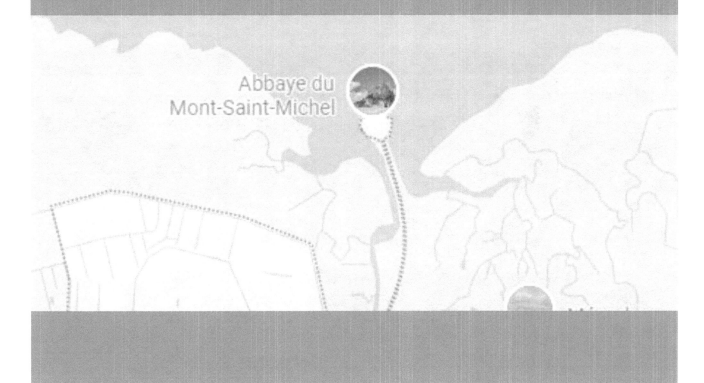

SCAN HERE HOW TO USE QR CODE

- Open your phone's camera app or download scanner app from play store or apple store
- Point the camera at the QR code for a few seconds (no need to take a photo).
- A link should appear on the display, leading you to the location of the code

Hauts-de-France

SCAN HERE

HOW TO USE QR CODE

- Open your phone's camera app or download scanner app from play store or apple store
- Point the camera at the QR code for a few seconds (no need to take a photo).
- A link should appear on the display, leading you to the location of the code

Lille

SCAN HERE

HOW TO USE QR CODE

- Open your phone's camera app or download scanner app from play store or apple store
- Point the camera at the QR code for a few seconds (no need to take a photo).
- A link should appear on the display, leading you to the location of the code

Eiffel Tower

SCAN HERE

HOW TO USE QR CODE

- Open your phone's camera app or download scanner app from play store or apple store
- Point the camera at the QR code for a few seconds (no need to take a photo).
- A link should appear on the display, leading you to the location of the code

Louvre Museum

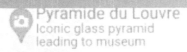

Pyramide du Louvre
Iconic glass pyramid
leading to museum

us les traits
rtius (copie)

Musée du Louvre

Louvre -

Cour Carrée

Mona Lisa)

Saint-Germa
Gra

Quai Francoi

Jardin de
l'Infante

SCAN HERE

HOW TO USE QR CODE

- Open your phone's camera app or download scanner app from play store or apple store
- Point the camera at the QR code for a few seconds (no need to take a photo).
- A link should appear on the display, leading you to the location of the code

Palace of Versailles

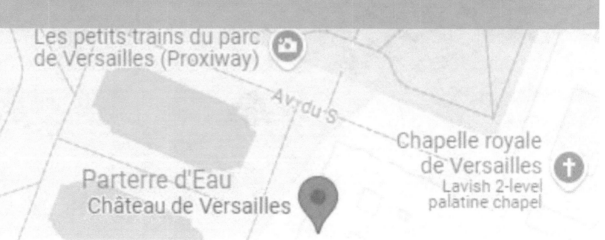

Les petits trains du parc de Versailles (Proxiway)

Av du S

Chapelle royale de Versailles
Lavish 2-level palatine chapel

Parterre d'Eau
Château de Versailles

La Loire

Cour Royale

SCAN HERE   HOW TO USE QR CODE

- Open your phone's camera app or download scanner app from play store or apple store
- Point the camera at the QR code for a few seconds (no need to take a photo).
- A link should appear on the display, leading you to the location of the code

Île-de-France

SCAN HERE HOW TO USE QR CODE

- Open your phone's camera app or download scanner app from play store or apple store
- Point the camera at the QR code for a few seconds (no need to take a photo).
- A link should appear on the display, leading you to the location of the code

provins

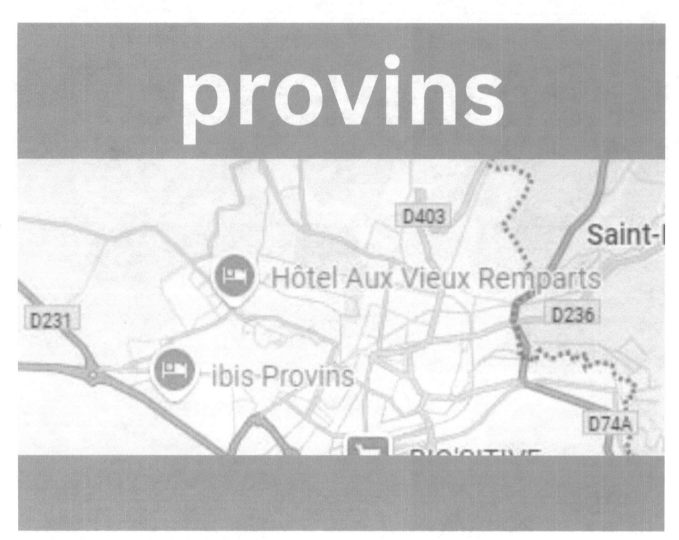

SCAN HERE

HOW TO USE QR CODE

- Open your phone's camera app or download scanner app from play store or apple store
- Point the camera at the QR code for a few seconds (no need to take a photo).
- A link should appear on the display, leading you to the location of the code

Alsace

SCAN HERE

HOW TO USE QR CODE

- Open your phone's camera app or download scanner app from play store or apple store
- Point the camera at the QR code for a few seconds (no need to take a photo).
- A link should appear on the display, leading you to the location of the code

Burgundy

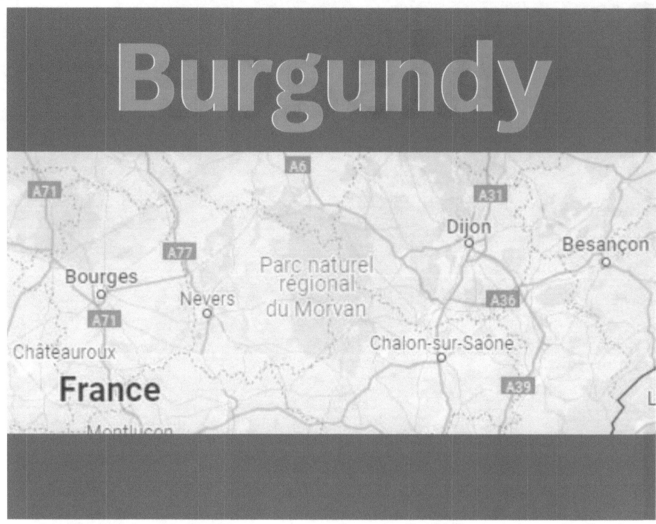

SCAN HERE

HOW TO USE QR CODE

- Open your phone's camera app or download scanner app from play store or apple store
- Point the camera at the QR code for a few seconds (no need to take a photo).
- A link should appear on the display, leading you to the location of the code

Rhone-Alpes

SCAN HERE

HOW TO USE QR CODE

- Open your phone's camera app or download scanner app from play store or apple store
- Point the camera at the QR code for a few seconds (no need to take a photo).
- A link should appear on the display, leading you to the location of the code

Lyon

SCAN HERE

HOW TO USE QR CODE

- Open your phone's camera app or download scanner app from play store or apple store
- Point the camera at the QR code for a few seconds (no need to take a photo).
- A link should appear on the display, leading you to the location of the code

Collonges-la-Rouge

SCAN HERE   HOW TO USE QR CODE

- Open your phone's camera app or download scanner app from play store or apple store
- Point the camera at the QR code for a few seconds (no need to take a photo).
- A link should appear on the display, leading you to the location of the code

Chapter 3

Iconic Road Trips across France

The Route des Grandes Alpes is an awe-inspiring road trip that captures the majestic beauty of the French Alps. Spanning over 720 kilometers, this legendary route connects Lake Geneva in the north to the Mediterranean Sea in the south. It is a must for travelers who love stunning landscapes, thrilling mountain passes, and the serenity of alpine villages.

1. Overview of the Route des Grandes Alpes

The journey is a scenic marvel, winding through 17 of the most breathtaking mountain passes in France, including iconic ones like the Col du Galibier and Col d'Izoard. These pathways showcase breathtaking vistas of rugged mountains, verdant valleys, and pristine glacial lakes.

Highlights of the Journey

Starting Point: Thonon-les-Bains on the shores of Lake Geneva.

Final Destination: Menton on the French Riviera, where the majestic Alps blend seamlessly with the Mediterranean.

Distance: Approximately 720 kilometers

Time Required: Plan for at least 5–7 days to fully experience the route, stopping at key locations along the way.

2. Planning Your Road Trip

Best Time to Visit

Summer (June to September): Ideal for a snow-free journey, offering clear skies and mild temperatures.

Autumn (September to October): For less crowds and colorful foliage.

Essential Preparations

Vehicle Tips: A reliable car with good brakes is crucial for navigating steep inclines and sharp turns.

What to Pack: Warm clothing, as temperatures can drop significantly at higher altitudes, even in summer.

3. Key Sections of the Route

Northern Section: From Lake Geneva to Megève

The tour begins at the spa town of Thonon-les-Bains, which is located on the banks of Lake Geneva.

Evian-les-Bains: Famous for its mineral water, this charming lakeside town is perfect for a shortstop.

Megève: A luxurious alpine village known for its charming chalets, cobblestone streets, and gourmet dining options.

Central Section: Through the Heart of the Alps

This stretch guides you through some of the route's most demanding yet rewarding sections.

Col de la Colombière: The first major mountain pass, offering panoramic views of the surrounding peaks.

Chamonix-Mont-Blanc: A detour to this world-famous ski resort is a must. From here, you can marvel at Mont Blanc, the highest peak in Western Europe.

Southern Section: From the Alps to the Riviera

As you head south, the landscape transitions from rugged mountains to rolling hills and, eventually, the sparkling Mediterranean.

Barcelonnette: A charming town showcasing a distinctive Mexican influence, reflected in its architecture and culinary offerings.

Menton: The journey concludes in this picturesque coastal town. Its pastel-colored buildings and citrus groves are a warm welcome to the Riviera.

4. Highlights along the Route

Stunning Natural Beauty

Lac d'Annecy: Often called Europe's cleanest lake, its turquoise waters are surrounded by mountains.

Mercantour National Park: A haven for wildlife, including ibex and marmots, with trails that allow you to stretch your legs and explore.

Charming Alpine Villages

La Grave: A tiny village offering incredible views of the La Meije Glacier.

Saint-Véran: Europe's highest inhabited village, where traditional wooden chalets and starry skies captivate visitors.

Cultural and Historical Gems

Fortresses and Castles: The Alps are dotted with historic forts, such as Fort Queyras, which provides insight into the region's military history.

Alpine Museums: Learn about the region's culture and traditions at museums in towns like Annecy and Gap.

5. Practical Tips for Travelers

Driving Considerations

Navigating Hairpin Turns: Drive cautiously, particularly on steep descents and sharp bends.

Toll Roads: Some sections may require toll payments, so carry cash or a credit card.

Accommodations

Alpine lodges: cozy, family-run lodges offer a warm and authentic experience.

Campsites: For nature lovers, campsites along the route provide stunning mountain vistas.

Local Cuisine

Regional Specialties: Savor dishes like raclette, fondue, and tartiflette—perfect comfort food for chilly alpine evenings.

Wines and Spirits: Enjoy local wines from the Rhône Valley and Chartreuse, an herbal liqueur crafted by monks.

6. Why This Road Trip is Unforgettable

The Route des Grandes Alpes is not just a journey through the mountains—it's an immersion into the heart of French culture and natural beauty. From the thrill of conquering high-altitude passes to the serenity of alpine meadows, this road trip offers a perfect blend of adventure and relaxation.

Memorable Experiences Watching the sunrise over Mont Blanc

Meandering through lavender fields tucked away at the foothills of the Alps.

Enjoying a Mediterranean sunset in Menton after days in the mountains.

Whether you're an experienced road tripper or embarking on your first alpine adventure, the Route des Grandes Alpes promises a journey of a lifetime. Start planning today, and let the magic of the French Alps guide your way to unforgettable memories!

The Wine Routes: A Journey through Alsace, Bordeaux, and Burgundy

France is synonymous with wine, and there's no better way to immerse yourself in its rich viticulture than by exploring its legendary wine routes. These journeys offer more than exceptional wine tastings—they provide a glimpse into the soul of French culture, where rolling vineyards, charming villages, and centuries-old traditions blend seamlessly.

1. The Alsace Wine Route: A Tale of Rieslings and Timeless Villages

Overview

The Alsace Wine Route, or Route des Vins d'Alsace, is one of France's most enchanting wine trails. Stretching over 170 kilometers from Thann to Marlenheim, it winds through picturesque villages, medieval castles, and rows of vineyards producing some of the finest Rieslings, Gewürztraminers, and Pinot Gris worldwide.

Key Highlights

Colmar: Often referred to as "Little Venice" due to its canals, Colmar is a picture-perfect town featuring vibrant half-timbered homes.

Château du Haut-Koenigsbourg: Situated on the Vosges mountains, this medieval fortress provides sweeping views of the nearby vineyards.

What to Savor

White Wines: Alsace is renowned for its aromatic whites, with Riesling leading the charge.

Cuisine Pairings: Sample tarte flambée, a thin-crust flatbread topped with cream, onions, and bacon, or choucroute garnie, a hearty dish of sauerkraut and sausages.

2. The Bordeaux Wine Route: Red Elegance and Coastal Beauty

Overview

The Bordeaux region is a dream destination for wine enthusiasts, renowned for creating some of the most esteemed red wines globally. With six primary wine trails, including the Médoc, Graves, and Saint-Émilion routes, this area offers a mix of modern vineyards and historic châteaux.

Key Highlights

Médoc Route: Home to legendary estates like Château Margaux and Château Latour, this trail is a journey through wine aristocracy.

Saint-Émilion: A UNESCO World Heritage Site, this medieval town is famed for its Merlots and breathtaking vineyards..

What to Savor

Red Wines: Bordeaux excels in blends dominated by Cabernet Sauvignon and Merlot.

Cuisine Pairings: Indulge in duck confit, foie gras, and canelés, a caramelized pastry unique to Bordeaux.

3. A Tour of Terroir along the Burgundy Wine Route

Overview

Burgundy also known as bourgogne, is the origin of Pinot Noir and Chardonnay. The Route des Grands Crus, stretching 60 kilometers between Dijon and Santenay, is a compact yet rich exploration of the region's winemaking legacy.

Key Highlights

Beaune: Known as the wine capital of Burgundy, Beaune boasts the historic Hôtel-Dieu, a 15th-century hospital turned museum.

Côte de Beaune: Renowned for its exquisite white wines, especially from towns such as Meursault and Puligny-Montrachet.

What to Savor

Red and White Wines: Burgundy's Pinot Noir is elegant and complex, while it's Chardonnay is rich and buttery.

Cuisine Pairings: Try boeuf bourguignon, a slow-cooked beef stew, and escargots (snails) in garlic butter.

The Normandy Coastline: A Journey of Natural Beauty and Historical Depth

The Normandy Coastline is a road trip like no other, combining stunning natural landscapes, charming seaside towns, and a profound sense of history. Stretching from Le Havre to Mont Saint-Michel, this route offers a diverse array of experiences—from towering cliffs to poignant WWII landmarks.

1. Natural Wonders along the Coast

The Alabaster Coast

Étretat: Famous for its dramatic white chalk cliffs and natural arches, Étretat is a painter's dream. Walk along the coastal trails to take in stunning vistas of the Falaise d'Aval and Falaise d'Amont.

Dieppe: A lively port town known for its pebble beaches, vibrant markets, and seafood restaurants.

The Cotentin Peninsula

Barfleur: A picturesque fishing village with granite houses and colorful boats.

Cap de la Hague: Often called "France's Land's End," this rugged promontory is a haven for hikers.

2. Historic Sites of Normandy

D-Day Beaches

Normandy's coastline is indelibly marked by its role in World War II.

Omaha Beach: Walk the sands where Allied forces landed on D-Day and visit the Normandy American Cemetery and Memorial.

Mont Saint-Michel

This famous island abbey, soaring strikingly from the ocean, is an essential place to visit. A UNESCO World Heritage Site, Mont Saint-Michel is both a spiritual retreat and a marvel of medieval engineering.

3. Practical Tips for Exploring the Normandy Coastline

Driving Tips: Many coastal roads are narrow and winding; drive cautiously, especially near cliffs.

Best Time to Visit: Spring and summer offer mild weather and vibrant blooms, while autumn provides quieter beaches and a cozy atmosphere.

Why These Routes Are Unmissable

Both the wine regions and the Normandy coastline offer unparalleled insights into the heart of France. Whether you're savoring a glass of vintage Bordeaux or standing on the windswept cliffs of Étretat, these journeys promise unforgettable memories.

The Dordogne valley An Exploration of historical heritage and Scenic Splendor.

The Dordogne Valley in southwestern France is a paradise for travelers seeking a blend of history, culture, and unspoiled landscapes. Known for its fairytale castles, prehistoric caves, and rolling countryside, the Dordogne is the epitome of rural charm. As you navigate its scenic roads, every turn reveals something extraordinary, making it an unforgettable road trip destination.

1. Scenic Routes through the Dordogne

The Castle Trail

The Dordogne has earned its nickname as the "Land of 1,001 Castles" for valid reasons. Driving along the Dordogne River unveils a procession of stunning medieval fortresses and elegant châteaux.

Château de Beynac: Offering stunning vistas and an insight into medieval life, this castle is perched high on a rock above the river.

Château des Milandes: Once home to Josephine Baker, this castle combines Renaissance architecture with a moving story of resilience and artistry.

The Prehistoric Route

The Dordogne Valley is one of the world's richest regions for prehistoric art and archaeological sites.

Lascaux Caves: Known as the "Sistine Chapel of Prehistory," these caves house intricate Paleolithic paintings. While the original cave is closed to the public, Lascaux IV, a state-of-the-art replica, offers an immersive experience.

Font-de-Gaume: This UNESCO-listed cave contains vivid polychrome paintings that have survived for thousands of years.

2. Culinary Delights along the Way

The Dordogne Valley is a gastronomic haven. While driving through the region, be sure to indulge in local delicacies:

Truffles: Known as "black diamonds," Dordogne truffles are a sought-after luxury. Visit a local truffle farm for a guided tasting.

Foie Gras: A staple of the region, this delicacy is best enjoyed with a glass of local wine.

Walnuts: The Dordogne is famed for its walnut orchards, offering everything from walnut oils to pastries like gâteau aux noix.

3. Practical Tips for Exploring the Dordogne Valley

Road Conditions: Many roads are narrow and winding. Drive cautiously, especially in rural areas.

Best Time to Visit: Spring and autumn are ideal for avoiding crowds and enjoying mild weather.

Accommodations: Opt for a stay in a traditional gîte (holiday home) for an authentic experience.

Corsica's Coastal Drive: A Mediterranean Dream

Corsica, often referred to as the "Island of Beauty," is a land of contrasts, offering rugged mountains, pristine beaches, and a distinct Mediterranean culture. A road trip along Corsica's coastal routes reveals dramatic cliffs, turquoise waters, and charming villages that blend French and Italian influences

1. The Highlights of Corsica's Coastal Drive

Calanques de Piana

A UNESCO World Heritage Site, the Calanques de Piana are dramatic red granite cliffs that plunge into the sea. The winding coastal road between Porto and Piana offers breathtaking views at every turn.

Photo Opportunities: Stop at scenic viewpoints like Capu Rossu for postcard-perfect shots.

The Scandola Nature Reserve

Accessible by road and boat, this reserve showcases Corsica's untamed beauty. Volcanic rock formations, secluded coves, and diverse marine life make it a must-see.

2. Corsican Culture along the Way

The food, language, and customs of Corsica reflect its distinctive fusion of French and Italian ancestry.

Local Specialties: Sample dishes like civet de sanglier (wild boar stew) and brocciu (a sheep's milk cheese).

Festivals: Time your visit to coincide with local events like the Fiera di u Vinu, celebrating Corsican wines.

3. Practical Tips for Corsica's Coastal Drive

Driving Conditions: Coastal roads can be narrow with sharp bends. Drive cautiously, especially in mountainous areas.

Ferries: If bringing your car, ferries connect Corsica to mainland France (Nice, Marseille) and Italy (Savona, Livorno).

Ideal Time to Visit: Spring and early summer provide enjoyable weather and smaller crowds.

Why These Routes Are Must-Experience Adventures

The Dordogne Valley and Corsica's coastal drives each offer something unique—whether it's the deep historical resonance of the Dordogne or the wild Mediterranean allure of Corsica. These routes promise an immersive journey through the heart and soul of France, leaving travelers with memories as rich as the landscapes themselves.

Start planning your adventure now and let France's stunning regions take your breath away!

Rte des Grandes Alpes

Rte des Grandes Alpes
D902

SCAN HERE

HOW TO USE QR CODE

- Open your phone's camera app or download scanner app from play store or apple store
- Point the camera at the QR code for a few seconds (no need to take a photo).
- A link should appear on the display, leading you to the location of the code

Col du Galibier

SCAN HERE

HOW TO USE QR CODE

- Open your phone's camera app or download scanner app from play store or apple store
- Point the camera at the QR code for a few seconds (no need to take a photo).
- A link should appear on the display, leading you to the location of the code

Col d'Izoard

Col d'Izoard

D902

SCAN HERE

HOW TO USE QR CODE

- Open your phone's camera app or download scanner app from play store or apple store
- Point the camera at the QR code for a few seconds (no need to take a photo).
- A link should appear on the display, leading you to the location of the code

Thonon-les-Bains

SCAN HERE

HOW TO USE QR CODE

- Open your phone's camera app or download scanner app from play store or apple store
- Point the camera at the QR code for a few seconds (no need to take a photo).
- A link should appear on the display, leading you to the location of the code

Lake Geneva

SCAN HERE

HOW TO USE QR CODE

- Open your phone's camera app or download scanner app from play store or apple store
- Point the camera at the QR code for a few seconds (no need to take a photo).
- A link should appear on the display, leading you to the location of the code

Megève

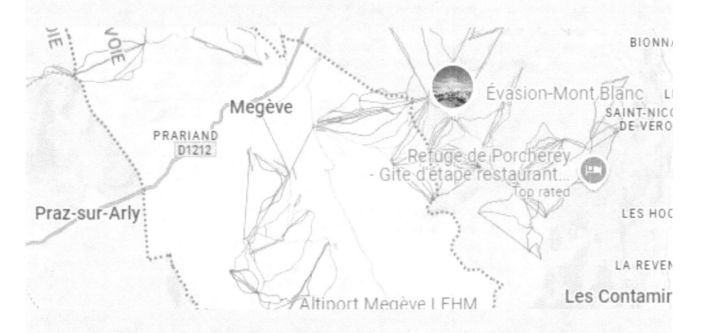

SCAN HERE

HOW TO USE QR CODE

- Open your phone's camera app or download scanner app from play store or apple store
- Point the camera at the QR code for a few seconds (no need to take a photo).
- A link should appear on the display, leading you to the location of the code

Col de la Colombière

Chalet de la Colombière

Col de la Colombière

SCAN HERE

HOW TO USE QR CODE

- Open your phone's camera app or download scanner app from play store or apple store
- Point the camera at the QR code for a few seconds (no need to take a photo).
- A link should appear on the display, leading you to the location of the code

Barcelonnette

Saint-Pons

Faucon-de-Barcelo

hotel SPA Azteca

Barcelonnette

D902

Camping La Chaup.
Temporarily closed

LA CONCHETTE

SCAN HERE

HOW TO USE QR CODE

- Open your phone's camera app or download scanner app from play store or apple store
- Point the camera at the QR code for a few seconds (no need to take a photo).
- A link should appear on the display, leading you to the location of the code

Menton

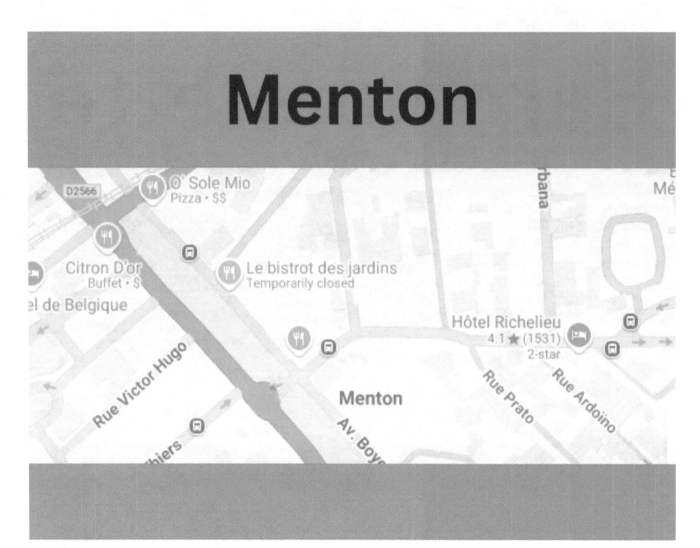

SCAN HERE

HOW TO USE QR CODE

- Open your phone's camera app or download scanner app from play store or apple store
- Point the camera at the QR code for a few seconds (no need to take a photo).
- A link should appear on the display, leading you to the location of the code

Lake Annecy

SCAN HERE

HOW TO USE QR CODE

- Open your phone's camera app or download scanner app from play store or apple store
- Point the camera at the QR code for a few seconds (no need to take a photo).
- A link should appear on the display, leading you to the location of the code

Saint-Véran

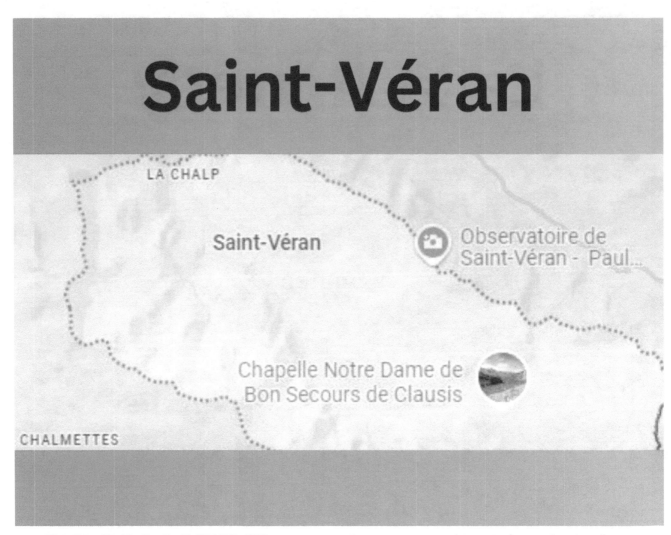

SCAN HERE

HOW TO USE QR CODE

- Open your phone's camera app or download scanner app from play store or apple store
- Point the camera at the QR code for a few seconds (no need to take a photo).
- A link should appear on the display, leading you to the location of the code

Route des Vins d'Alsace

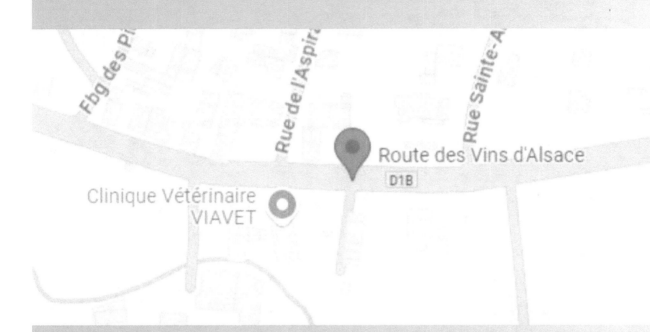

SCAN HERE

HOW TO USE QR CODE

- Open your phone's camera app or download scanner app from play store or apple store
- Point the camera at the QR code for a few seconds (no need to take a photo).
- A link should appear on the display, leading you to the location of the code

Saint-Émilion

SCAN HERE

HOW TO USE QR CODE

- Open your phone's camera app or download scanner app from play store or apple store
- Point the camera at the QR code for a few seconds (no need to take a photo).
- A link should appear on the display, leading you to the location of the code

Normandy

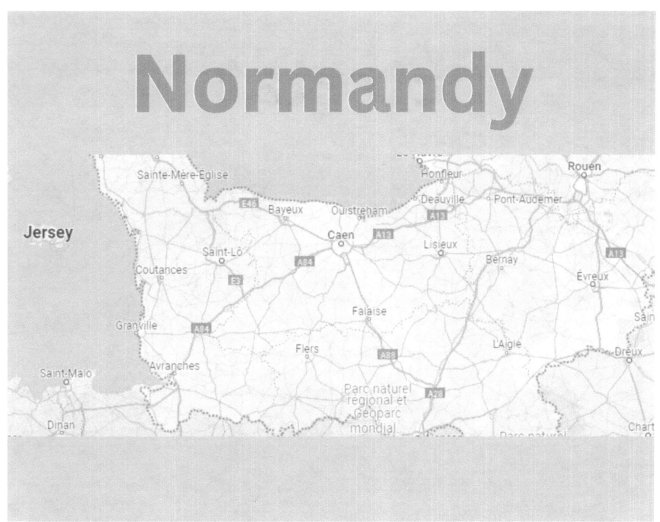

SCAN HERE

HOW TO USE QR CODE

- Open your phone's camera app or download scanner app from play store or apple store
- Point the camera at the QR code for a few seconds (no need to take a photo).
- A link should appear on the display, leading you to the location of the code

Étretat

SCAN HERE

HOW TO USE QR CODE

- Open your phone's camera app or download scanner app from play store or apple store
- Point the camera at the QR code for a few seconds (no need to take a photo).
- A link should appear on the display, leading you to the location of the code

Mont Saint-Michel

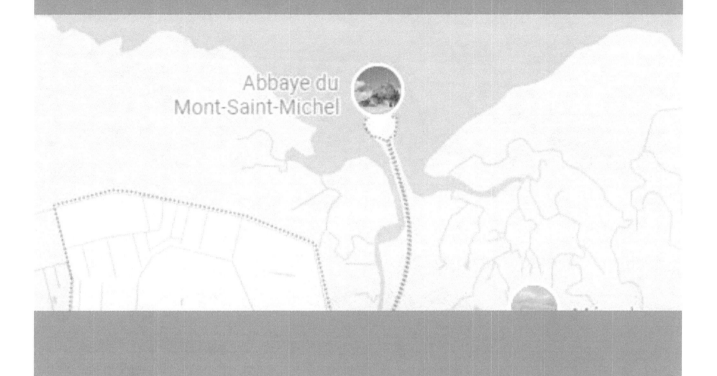

SCAN HERE

HOW TO USE QR CODE

- Open your phone's camera app or download scanner app from play store or apple store
- Point the camera at the QR code for a few seconds (no need to take a photo).
- A link should appear on the display, leading you to the location of the code

Dordogne

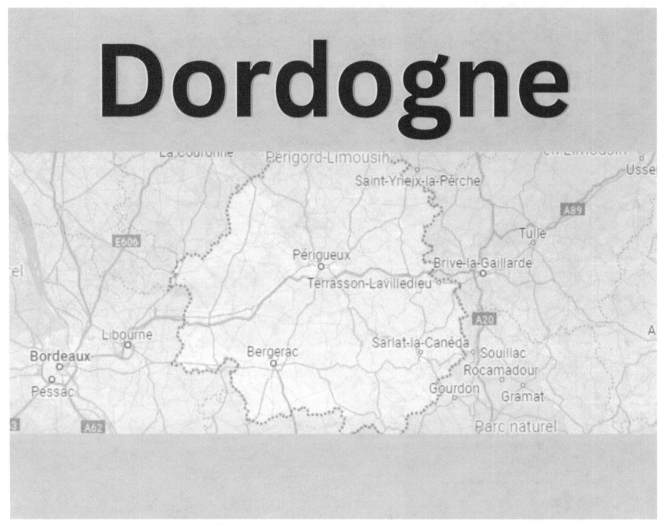

SCAN HERE

HOW TO USE QR CODE

- Open your phone's camera app or download scanner app from play store or apple store
- Point the camera at the QR code for a few seconds (no need to take a photo).
- A link should appear on the display, leading you to the location of the code

Château de Beynac

SCAN HERE

HOW TO USE QR CODE

- Open your phone's camera app or download scanner app from play store or apple store
- Point the camera at the QR code for a few seconds (no need to take a photo).
- A link should appear on the display, leading you to the location of the code

Lascaux

SCAN HERE

HOW TO USE QR CODE

- Open your phone's camera app or download scanner app from play store or apple store
- Point the camera at the QR code for a few seconds (no need to take a photo).
- A link should appear on the display, leading you to the location of the code

Corsica

SCAN HERE

HOW TO USE QR CODE

- Open your phone's camera app or download scanner app from play store or apple store
- Point the camera at the QR code for a few seconds (no need to take a photo).
- A link should appear on the display, leading you to the location of the code

Auberge du Sanglier

SCAN HERE

HOW TO USE QR CODE

- Open your phone's camera app or download scanner app from play store or apple store
- Point the camera at the QR code for a few seconds (no need to take a photo).
- A link should appear on the display, leading you to the location of the code

Nice

SCAN HERE

HOW TO USE QR CODE

- Open your phone's camera app or download scanner app from play store or apple store
- Point the camera at the QR code for a few seconds (no need to take a photo).
- A link should appear on the display, leading you to the location of the code

Chapter 4

Driving Laws and Regulations in France (2025 Update)

Navigating the roads of France requires an understanding of the country's driving laws and regulations. This section provides a comprehensive overview of the general rules of the road, ensuring that travelers can explore France confidently and safely. The 2025 updates reflect changes in speed limits, documentation requirements, and safety protocols that all drivers should know.

1. General Rules of the Road in France

Driving in France can be straightforward if you familiarize yourself with the basic rules. **Here's what every motorist needs to know**

Speed Limits

In France, speed limits are influenced by the kind of road, the weather, and the driver's condition.

Autoroutes (Highways)

Normal conditions: 130 km/h (81 mph).

Wet conditions: 110 km/h (68 mph).

For drivers holding a license for less than three years 110 km/h (68 mph) regardless of weather.

National Roads

Normal conditions: 80 km/h (50 mph).

Wet conditions: 70 km/h (43 mph).

Urban Areas

Default limit: 50 km/h (31 mph). Some residential areas enforce lower limits of 30 km/h (18 mph).

Speed cameras are common, and exceeding the limit can lead to hefty fines, points on your license, or even confiscation of your vehicle for serious infractions.

Seatbelt Laws

Every passenger in a car must wear a seatbelt, regardless of where they sit.

The penalty for noncompliance is €135.

Children under 10 must travel in an approved child seat or booster, appropriate for their weight and height.

Cellphone Usage

Using a mobile phone while driving is strictly prohibited unless you're using a completely hands-free system.

Holding or handling a phone, even when stationary, can lead to a fine of €135 and the loss of three points on a French driving license.

Headsets and earphones are also banned, emphasizing the need for distraction-free driving.

2. Requirements for International Drivers

France welcomes millions of international travelers each year, many of whom opt to explore by car. To drive legally in France as a foreigner, you'll need to meet the following requirements:

International Driving Permit (IDP)

EU/EEA Drivers: A valid driving license from an EU or EEA country is sufficient. No IDP is needed.

Non-EU/EEA Drivers: Most travelers, including those from the United States, Canada, and Australia, need an IDP along with their domestic license. Check with local French embassies to confirm requirements.

Vehicle Insurance

Every vehicle driven in France must have valid third-party liability insurance (also known as assurance au tiers).

Many rental car companies include basic insurance, but it's wise to confirm coverage and consider additional policies for peace of mind.

Always have evidence of insurance in the vehicle.

Required Documents

A valid driver's license

Vehicle registration documents

Insurance certificate

For rentals: The rental agreement and proof of payment.

Failure to produce these documents during a police stop could result in fines or delays.

3. Other Essential Rules

Priority to the Right (Priorité à Droite)

This rule is a hallmark of French driving law, particularly in rural areas and small towns.

Unless signs or road markings specify otherwise, vehicles arriving from the right always have priority at unmarked crossroads. Not yielding when necessary can lead to accidents or result in fines.

Roundabouts

Navigating roundabouts in France follows a straightforward rule:

Traffic inside the roundabout has priority unless otherwise marked.

Drivers must yield to oncoming traffic when they enter a roundabout.

Alcohol Limits

France enforces strict blood alcohol limits to ensure road safety:

0.05% BAC (50 mg of alcohol per 100 ml of blood) is the standard driver.

New or young drivers: 0.02% BAC (20 mg of alcohol per 100 ml of blood).

Penalties for exceeding these limits range from fines to immediate license suspension or criminal charges for severe offenses.

Winter Driving Laws

Some areas in France now mandate the use of winter tires or snow chains during the winter season, from November 1 to March 31. These areas include mountainous regions such as the Alps, Pyrenees, and Massif Central. Ensure your vehicle complies if traveling during these periods.

4. Penalties and Fines

French authorities enforce driving laws stringently, with on-the-spot fines for certain violations.

Speeding: Fines range from €68 to €1,500, depending on severity.

Running a Red Light: A fine of €135 and potential license suspension.

Driving without a Seatbelt: €135 fine.

Failure to Yield: Fines start at €135.

Fines for foreign drivers must typically be paid immediately. Police officers may confiscate the vehicle if payment cannot be made.

5. Practical Tips for a Smooth Driving Experience

Know the Signs: Familiarize yourself with French road signs, many of which are unique and rely heavily on symbols rather than text.

Plan for Tolls: Carry a mix of cash and a credit card, as some toll booths may not accept all cards.

Use Rest Stops: France's autoroutes offer excellent aires (rest areas) equipped with picnic spots, fuel stations, and even play areas for children.

Driving in France can be a rewarding experience, offering freedom and access to stunning destinations. You'll be ready for a fun and safe road trip if you keep these rules in mind.

France's extensive network of toll roads, or autoroutes, makes traveling between regions swift and efficient. However, understanding how tolls work and exploring alternative routes can help you make informed decisions about your journey.

1. Understanding Toll Roads in France

France's toll roads are among the best-maintained in Europe, providing smooth rides and facilities like rest areas, fuel stations, and restaurants.

How Toll Costs are calculated

Tolls in France are calculated based on

Distance Traveled: You will pay more the longer you travel on a toll road.

Vehicle Category: Tolls differ depending on the type of vehicle:

Class 1: Cars, motorcycles, and small vans.

Class 2: Motorhomes and larger vans.

Class 3: Trucks and vehicles with two axles over 3.5 tons.

Class 4: Heavy goods vehicles and buses.

Class 5: Motorcycles with sidecars or trailers.

Payment Methods

Toll booths in France are equipped with multiple payment options for convenience:

Credit/Debit Cards: Most toll booths accept cards, but ensure your card has a chip and PIN. Some booths may not accept foreign cards, so it's wise to carry alternatives.

Cash: Euros are widely accepted, but having exact change speeds up the process.

Electronic Toll Tags (Télépéage): Ideal for frequent travelers, the Liber-t tag allows seamless access through toll gates in the designated lanes, with payments automatically debited.

Estimating Costs

To calculate toll expenses for your journey

Use online tools like ViaMichelin or Autoroutes.fr, which provide detailed breakdowns of toll fees and alternative routes.

For example, driving from Paris to Marseille (775 km) costs approximately €60 for Class 1 vehicles.

2. Alternatives to Toll Roads

Toll roads are not the only way to explore France. If you prefer to avoid tolls:

National Roads (Routes Nationales):

These roads are toll-free and often pass through picturesque villages and towns, offering a slower but scenic journey.

Example: Route Nationale 7, known as the "Route of Holidays," is a charming alternative to autoroutes.

Departmental Roads (Routes Départementales):

These smaller roads provide a more immersive experience of rural France but may require careful navigation due to narrower paths and limited signage.

Planning Tools

Most GPS systems and apps like Google Maps or Waze allow you to choose routes that avoid toll roads.

3. Zones à Faibles Émissions, or ZFE, are areas with low emissions.

France is committed to reducing vehicular pollution, particularly in urban areas. As a result, low-emission zones, or Zones à Faibles Émissions (ZFE), have been introduced across the country. These areas limit entry for specific vehicles according to their emission levels.

Environmental Zones: How They Work

Cities with Environmental Zones

Major cities like Paris, Lyon, and Marseille, enforce ZFE restrictions. Vehicles entering these zones must display a Crit'Air vignette, a sticker indicating the vehicle's pollution level.

Crit'Air Sticker System

The Crit'Air sticker scheme classifies vehicles into six categories, ranging from Crit'Air 1 (the least polluting) to Crit'Air 6 (the most polluting).

Crit'Air 1: Electric and hydrogen vehicles.

Crit'Air 2: Hybrid and gas-powered cars.

Crit'Air 3-6: Diesel vehicles, older gas vehicles, and those with higher emissions.

Obtaining a Crit'Air Sticker

To obtain a Crit'Air sticker:

Visit the official Crit'Air website (certificate-air.gouv.fr).

Provide details about your vehicle, including registration documents.

Pay the small fee (approximately €5 for domestic applications and slightly higher for international ones).

Allow a few weeks for delivery, especially for international requests.

Non-Compliance Penalties

Vehicles without the appropriate Crit'Air sticker may be fined €68 to €135 depending on the city and offense. Always check the ZFE restrictions of your destination before traveling.

Navigating Environmental Zones

Temporary Restrictions

Some cities enforce ZFE rules only during high pollution periods. These restrictions are announced in advance, so staying updated is crucial.

ZFE-Compatible Routes:

Most navigation apps now include settings to guide you through routes that comply with ZFE regulations.

Long-Term Planning

The French government is expanding the ZFE program to include more cities by 2030, making eco-friendly driving increasingly important.

Practical Tips for Navigating Toll Roads and Environmental Zones

Plan Ahead

Calculate toll costs and check ZFE rules before starting your journey. Online tools and travel apps can save you time and stress.

Keep Change Handy

While electronic payments dominate, having coins or small bills is always helpful, especially at older toll booths.

Eco-Friendly Rentals

If renting a car, opt for a hybrid or electric vehicle to minimize emissions and meet ZFE requirements effortlessly.

Understanding the toll systems and environmental regulations allows you to navigate France's roads smoothly, whether you're exploring bustling cities or scenic countryside routes.

Traffic Offenses and Penalties

Understanding traffic regulations and the consequences of breaking them is essential for a hassle-free journey through France. These are common traffic offenses, their penalties, and how to handle encounters with law enforcement.

1. Common Traffic Offenses and Fines

France has strict traffic laws to ensure road safety and discipline. Visitors should be aware of the following offenses to avoid penalties:

Speeding

Speeding Penalties: Speed limits are strictly enforced using fixed cameras, mobile radar, and unmarked police vehicles.

Minor infractions (less than 20 km/h over the limit): Fine of €68 in urban areas or €135 on highways.

Severe infractions (more than 50 km/h over the limit): Fine of up to €1,500, license suspension, and possible vehicle confiscation.

Avoiding Speeding Tickets

Stay alert to posted speed limits, often reduced in poor weather.

Use GPS or apps like Waze to detect speed traps and cameras (legal in France as long as they're not live radar warnings).

Disregarding stop signs and red lights

Running a red light incurs a fine of €135 and may result in points deducted from your driving record.

Using a Mobile Phone While Driving

Using a handheld device while driving is illegal, even when stopped at traffic lights.

Penalty: Fine of €135 and the possible suspension of your license for non-residents. Hands-free kits are allowed but discouraged.

Alcohol and Drug Driving Laws

Legal Blood Alcohol Limit: 0.05% (0.02% for new drivers with less than three years of experience).

Penalties for exceeding the limit

A fine of €135 to €4,500.

Immediate license suspension and possible imprisonment for severe offenses.

Zero tolerance exists for drug-impaired driving, with similar penalties.

Improper Parking

Parking in prohibited zones, such as pedestrian crossings or bike lanes, results in a fine of €35 to €135. Your vehicle could be towed if it hinders traffic flow.

Not Wearing a Seatbelt

Seatbelts are mandatory for all passengers. Fines of €135 apply to the driver for violations by anyone in the car.

2. What to Do If Stopped by Police

Being stopped by law enforcement in France may seem intimidating, especially for foreign drivers. Here's how to handle such situations with confidence:

Stay Calm and Polite

Police in France are generally courteous and expect the same in return. Depending on the time of day, you can greet them with "Bonjour" or "Bonsoir."

Documents to Provide

Always carry the following documents

Verify the validity of your driver's license in France or if it is supported by an International Driving Permit (IDP).

Vehicle Registration (Carte Grise): If you're driving a rented car, this will be provided by the rental agency.

Insurance Certificate: Mandatory for all vehicles on French roads.

Passport: For identity verification if you're a foreign national.

Handling On-the-Spot Fines

In France, police can issue on-the-spot fines for traffic offenses.

Payment can often be made via card, but some situations may require cash, especially in rural areas.

If you disagree with the fine, you can request a formal dispute, but this must be handled through proper channels, often requiring legal assistance.

Dealing with Language Barriers

French police may not always speak fluent English. Keeping a translation app or phrasebook handy can help bridge communication gaps.

3. Strategies to Avoid Traffic Offenses

Familiarize Yourself with Rules:

Review the local traffic regulations before you hit the road. Utilize travel apps or guides to familiarize yourself with regional differences.

Plan Ahead

Unfamiliar roads can lead to accidental violations. GPS systems with pre-set navigation reduce the chance of breaking rules.

Rest and Focus

Fatigue is a leading cause of traffic accidents. Take breaks every two hours and avoid driving at night if you're feeling tired.

Be Vigilant

Watch for signage, particularly in urban areas where regulations can change abruptly.

Key Takeaways for Travelers

Be Proactive: Learn the rules before your trip and keep a list of emergency contacts.

Stay Equipped: Carry required documents and items like reflective vests, warning triangles, and breathalyzers (mandatory in France).

Resolve Issues Promptly: If you receive a fine, pay it or address it through the official process promptly to avoid further complications.

By respecting traffic laws and staying prepared, you can ensure a smooth and enjoyable driving experience in France. Whether cruising along coastal roads or exploring charming villages, understanding and following the rules will help you travel with peace of mind.

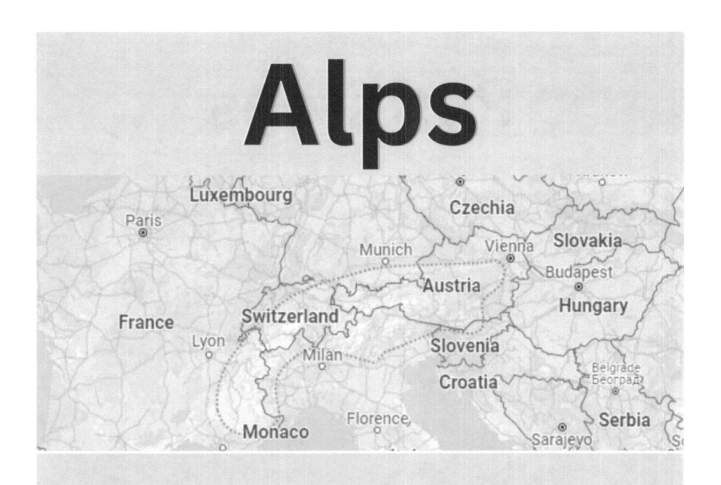

Alps

SCAN HERE

HOW TO USE QR CODE

- Open your phone's camera app or download scanner app from play store or apple store
- Point the camera at the QR code for a few seconds (no need to take a photo).
- A link should appear on the display, leading you to the location of the code

Pyrenees

Map of the Pyrenees region showing Bordeaux, Bergerac, Parc naturel régional des Landes de Gascogne, Agen, Montauban, Albi, Parc naturel régional de l'Aubrac, Parc naturel régional des Grands Causses, Auch, Toulouse, Béziers, Pau, Tarbes, Carcassonne, and highways A63, A62, A65, A64, A61, A75, A9.

SCAN HERE

HOW TO USE QR CODE

- Open your phone's camera app or download scanner app from play store or apple store
- Point the camera at the QR code for a few seconds (no need to take a photo).
- A link should appear on the display, leading you to the location of the code

Paris

SCAN HERE

HOW TO USE QR CODE

- Open your phone's camera app or download scanner app from play store or apple store
- Point the camera at the QR code for a few seconds (no need to take a photo).
- A link should appear on the display, leading you to the location of the code

Lyon

SCAN HERE

HOW TO USE QR CODE

- Open your phone's camera app or download scanner app from play store or apple store
- Point the camera at the QR code for a few seconds (no need to take a photo).
- A link should appear on the display, leading you to the location of the code

Marseille

SCAN HERE

HOW TO USE QR CODE

- Open your phone's camera app or download scanner app from play store or apple store
- Point the camera at the QR code for a few seconds (no need to take a photo).
- A link should appear on the display, leading you to the location of the code

Chapter 5

Accommodations and Amenities for Road Trippers

Best Places to Stay Along the Road

Traveling through France by car offers unparalleled freedom, allowing you to discover its vast landscapes at your own pace. However, where you stay each night is as crucial as the journey itself. From charming hotels and cozy guesthouses to budget-friendly roadside motels and picturesque camping sites, France caters to every type of traveler.

1. Hotels and Guesthouses: A Taste of French Hospitality

France is renowned for its diverse accommodations that reflect its regional culture. Travelers can find luxurious city hotels, quaint rural inns, and boutique guesthouses across the country.

Hotels

City Hotels: Perfect for urban explorers, these accommodations often include modern amenities, proximity to landmarks, and multilingual staff.

Recommendations

Paris: Hôtel du Louvre for its central location and views of the iconic museum.

Lyon: Villa Florentine, offering stunning panoramas and gourmet dining.

Regional Charm: Many smaller towns boast hotels infused with local culture.

For example, the Hôtel de la Cité in Carcassonne is located within the medieval citadel.

Guesthouses (Chambres d'Hôtes)

For a more personal experience, guesthouses allow travelers to connect with local hosts.

Benefits

Authentic experiences, often including home-cooked meals.

Hosts offer helpful recommendations on the best local sites and restaurants.

Recommended Areas

Alsace: Stay in half-timbered homes surrounded by vineyards.

Provence: Enjoy the rustic allure of lavender fields as your stunning backdrop.

2. Roadside Motels and Budget Accommodations

When driving long distances, especially on autoroutes (French highways), roadside motels and budget-friendly options can be a practical choice.

Roadside Motels

These are ideal for short stays during multi-day road trips.

Features:

Parking facilities, basic amenities, and easy highway access.

Chains like ibis Budget and Première Classe offer consistent standards.

Youth Hostels

Budget-conscious travelers can opt for hostels, which are plentiful in France.

Modern hostels often feature private rooms, free Wi-Fi, and communal areas.

Example: The Generator Hostel in Paris, a vibrant option with rooftop views of Montmartre.

3. Camping and Caravaning: A Close-to-Nature Option

France is a haven for outdoor enthusiasts, with camping and caravaning being popular among road trippers.

Camping Sites

From basic pitches to luxury glamping sites, camping options abound.

Top Regions for Camping

Brittany: Seaside campsites offer proximity to dramatic coastlines.

Dordogne: Campsites are often nestled near rivers and castles.

Essential Tips for Campers

Book in advance during peak summer months.

Look for sites rated with the Camping Qualité label, ensuring high standards.

Caravaning (RV Travel)

France's aires de camping-car (RV-friendly areas) makes it easy to explore by motorhome.

Features include

Dedicated parking, waste disposal, and water refill stations.

Many are located near tourist hotspots or scenic areas.

Popular routes include

The Loire Valley: Park near historic châteaux.

The Côte d'Azur: Delight in seaside locations with beach access.

4. Booking Tips and Insights

To ensure a stress-free stay, consider the following

When to Book

Peak Season: Summer (June to August) sees higher demand, especially in tourist-heavy areas like Provence and the Côte d'Azur. Book accommodations months in advance during this period.

Off-Season: Late fall and winter offer better rates and availability.

Platforms and Resources

Hotels: Websites like Booking.com and Expedia allow you to filter by budget and amenities.

Guesthouses: Use platforms like Gîtes de France for authentic stays.

Camping: Eurocamp and CampingFrance.com provide comprehensive listings.

Cancellation Policies

Look for accommodations with flexible cancellation options, especially if your road trip plans may change.

5. Essential Amenities to Consider

When choosing places to stay, make sure they meet the requirements of your road trip:

Secure Parking: A must for urban stays or areas with limited street parking.

Wi-Fi Access: Essential for planning routes and checking local attractions.

On-Site Dining: Convenient for remote areas or after a long drive.

Pet-Friendly Options: If traveling with pets, confirm whether accommodations welcome them.

Key Takeaways for Travelers

France offers diverse accommodations tailored to various preferences and budgets.

Research and planning are vital, especially during high-demand seasons.

Mix traditional hotels with unique stays for a well-rounded experience.

Wherever the road leads you, selecting the right accommodations will enhance your journey through France, ensuring you wake up refreshed and ready to explore the next destination.

Dining on the Road

France is synonymous with world-class cuisine, and road-tripping through this gastronomic paradise provides the perfect opportunity to savor its diverse culinary offerings. Each region has its distinctive flavors, local specialties, and dining traditions, ensuring that every meal is a memorable part of your journey. Whether you're stopping at a roadside bistro, indulging in a Michelin-starred restaurant, or sampling fresh produce from a local market, dining in France enriches the travel experience.

1. Local Specialties by Region

France's diverse cuisine showcases its varied landscapes and cultural traditions. As you travel across the country, exploring these distinctive dishes enables you to experience the authentic essence of each region.

Northern France

Normandy

Must-Try Dishes

Camembert: A rich, creamy cheese that originates from the area.

Seafood: Fresh oysters and mussels, usually served with robust bread.

Apple-based Desserts: Tarte Tatin and Calvados-infused treats.

Top Spot: Visit Honfleur for seaside dining featuring local seafood.

Hauts-de-France

Staples

Welsh Rarebit: A hearty cheese and beer dish served on bread.

Moules-frites: Mussels paired with crispy French fries.

Beer: Regional craft brews are a must-try.

Top Spot: Lille's historic brasseries are excellent for traditional meals.

Western France

Brittany

Galettes and crêpes: buckwheat pancakes stuffed with cheese, ham, or seafood.

Seafood: Fresh langoustines, lobster, and scallops from coastal towns.

Cider: Brittany's artisanal ciders are the perfect pairing.

Top Spot: Saint-Malo, for fresh seafood in a historic walled city setting.

Loire Valley

Delights

Goat Cheese: Chèvre from the region is legendary.

Tarte Tatin: Originating here, this caramelized apple pie is a must.

Wines: Sample crisp Sauvignon Blanc and fruity Cabernet Franc.

Top Spot: Amboise, where charming riverside restaurants pair châteaux views with fine dining.

Southern France

Provence

Provençal Specialties:

Bouillabaisse: A rich seafood stew from Marseille.

Tapenade: Olive-based spreads perfect with fresh bread.

Lavender Desserts: Unique pastries and ice creams flavored with local lavender.

Top Spot: Aix-en-Provence offers vibrant farmers' markets and chic bistros.

Côte d'Azur

Mediterranean Flavors:

Ratatouille: A vegetable stew seasoned with herbs de Provence.

Niçoise Salad: A fresh, balanced dish combining tuna, olives, and vegetables.

Rosé Wines: Crisp and refreshing, ideal for the coastal climate.

Top Spot: Nice, where open-air cafés serve authentic Provençal meals.

Eastern France

Alsace

Alsatian Cuisine

Choucroute Garnie: Sauerkraut served with sausages and pork.

Flammkuchen: A light, crisp flatbread topped with crème fraîche, onions, and bacon.

Wine: Known for Riesling and Gewürztraminer.

Top Spot: Strasbourg, where traditional winstubs (wine taverns) serve authentic fare.

Burgundy

Wine and Gastronomy

Beef Bourguignon: A hearty beef stew cooked slowly in Burgundy wine.

Escargots: Snails prepared with garlic butter.

Top Spot: Beaune, the wine capital of Burgundy, for vineyard-to-table dining.

2. Tips for Finding Authentic Restaurants and Rest Stops

Dining Like a Local

Avoid tourist traps by seeking out establishments frequented by locals.

Explore beyond the usual routes for a taste of more authentic dishes.

Best Tools for Discovery

Travel Apps: Use apps like Yelp, TripAdvisor, or TheFork to find reviews and recommendations.

Ask the Locals: Hotel staff, guesthouse hosts, and even locals at markets can offer valuable suggestions.

Rest Stops on Highways

Autoroute Stops: French motorways (autoroutes) often feature Aires de Service, which are rest areas with excellent amenities.

2. Essential Dining Etiquette in France

Understanding French dining customs can enhance your culinary journey

Timing: Lunch is typically served between 12 PM and 2 PM, and dinner starts around 7 PM. Restaurants may close outside these hours.

Tipping: Service fees are generally included in the total, but it is appreciated if you round up or leave some spare change.

Reservations: Always book ahead for popular restaurants, especially in cities.

3. Packing Snacks and Planning for Meals

Grocery Stores and Markets

Stock up on fresh baguettes, cheeses, cured meats, and fruits at local markets for road trip picnics.

Chain supermarkets like Carrefour and Intermarché are convenient for essentials.

Portable Coolers

A cooler or insulated bag can keep perishable items fresh during long drives.

Hydration

Always have bottled water on hand, especially when traveling during the warmer months.

Key Takeaways for Road Trippers

France's culinary diversity ensures delightful dining experiences throughout your journey.

Plan meals around local specialties and seek out hidden gems for authentic tastes.

Enjoy a mix of sit-down meals, market finds, and scenic picnics for a well-rounded gastronomic adventure.

With thoughtful planning and an appetite for exploration, dining on the road becomes a highlight of your French road trip, adding delicious memories to your travels.

Sufficient planning for refueling is vital for an enjoyable and seamless road trip across France. Understanding the types of fuel available, associated costs, and payment options can help ensure uninterrupted travel. Moreover, with the rise in electric vehicle (EV) adoption, access to charging infrastructure is becoming increasingly important for eco-conscious travelers.

1. Fuel Types in France

French fuel stations cater to a variety of vehicle types, ensuring drivers can find the right option for their car:

Common Fuel Types

Diesel (Gazole):

Widely available and slightly cheaper than gasoline.

Preferred by many European vehicles due to efficiency and cost benefits.

Unleaded Gasoline (Sans Plomb)

SP95: Standard unleaded fuel.

SP98: A premium variant with higher octane levels, suitable for high-performance engines.

E10 (Biofuel Blend):

A mix of gasoline and bioethanol is available at most stations.

Typically less expensive but may not be suitable for older cars.

LPG (Liquefied Petroleum Gas)

A greener and more economical alternative.

Not as commonly available as diesel or gasoline, so plan if using an LPG vehicle.

Tips for Selecting the Right Fuel

Double-check your car's fuel requirements, as mistakenly refueling with the wrong type can damage the engine.

Fuel nozzles are color-coded but confirm with station signage to avoid confusion.

2. Fuel Costs and Payment Methods

Fuel Costs in 2025

Price Variations: Fuel prices fluctuate based on global oil markets, regional taxes, and the station's location.

Highways: Expect higher prices at autoroute service areas due to convenience and limited competition.

Rural Areas: Often slightly cheaper but may have fewer stations.

Average Prices: In 2025, diesel and E10 are generally more affordable than SP95 or SP98.

Payment Options

Credit and Debit Cards

Most stations accept Visa and MasterCard.

Some automated pumps require chip-enabled cards and may not accept foreign-issued cards without a PIN.

Cash

Useful at smaller, independently operated stations or in rural areas.

Be aware that automated pumps typically do not accept cash.

Prepaid Fuel Cards

A convenient option for frequent travelers in France, available for purchase at major stations.

3. Navigating Fuel Stations

Station Types

Highway Service Areas (Aires de Service)

Located at regular intervals along autoroutes.

Offer 24/7 fuel services, dining options, and basic vehicle maintenance supplies.

Local Stations

Found in cities, towns, and along departmental roads.

May have limited operating hours, particularly in smaller towns or during holidays.

Tips for Refueling

Plan Ahead: In remote regions, fuel stations may be sparse, so top up whenever the tank reaches half-full..

Avoid Last-Minute Refueling: Waiting until the fuel gauge is near empty can lead to unnecessary stress, especially in rural or mountainous areas.

4. EV Charging Stations for Electric Vehicles

With the push toward sustainability, France has developed an extensive network of EV charging stations to support electric vehicles.

Where to Find EV Charging Stations

Autoroutes and Major Roads

Highway Service Areas: Most aires de service now features fast-charging stations compatible with common EV models.

Popular operators include Ionity, TotalEnergies, and Tesla Superchargers.

Rural and Scenic Routes

Charging infrastructure is expanding, but availability may still be limited in remote regions. Use apps to pre-plan stops.

Leverage apps and modern payment options for seamless fuel management.

With careful preparation, your journey through France will remain efficient and enjoyable, ensuring that your focus stays on the stunning landscapes and memorable experiences along the way.

Hôtel du Louvre

SCAN HERE

HOW TO USE QR CODE

- Open your phone's camera app or download scanner app from play store or apple store
- Point the camera at the QR code for a few seconds (no need to take a photo).
- A link should appear on the display, leading you to the location of the code

Villa Florentine

SCAN HERE

HOW TO USE QR CODE

- Open your phone's camera app or download scanner app from play store or apple store
- Point the camera at the QR code for a few seconds (no need to take a photo).
- A link should appear on the display, leading you to the location of the code

Hotel de la Cite

SCAN HERE

HOW TO USE QR CODE

- Open your phone's camera app or download scanner app from play store or apple store
- Point the camera at the QR code for a few seconds (no need to take a photo).
- A link should appear on the display, leading you to the location of the code

Alsace

SCAN HERE

HOW TO USE QR CODE

- Open your phone's camera app or download scanner app from play store or apple store
- Point the camera at the QR code for a few seconds (no need to take a photo).
- A link should appear on the display, leading you to the location of the code

Generator Paris

SCAN HERE

HOW TO USE QR CODE

- Open your phone's camera app or download scanner app from play store or apple store
- Point the camera at the QR code for a few seconds (no need to take a photo).
- A link should appear on the display, leading you to the location of the code

Brittany

SCAN HERE

HOW TO USE QR CODE

- Open your phone's camera app or download scanner app from play store or apple store
- Point the camera at the QR code for a few seconds (no need to take a photo).
- A link should appear on the display, leading you to the location of the code

Dordogne

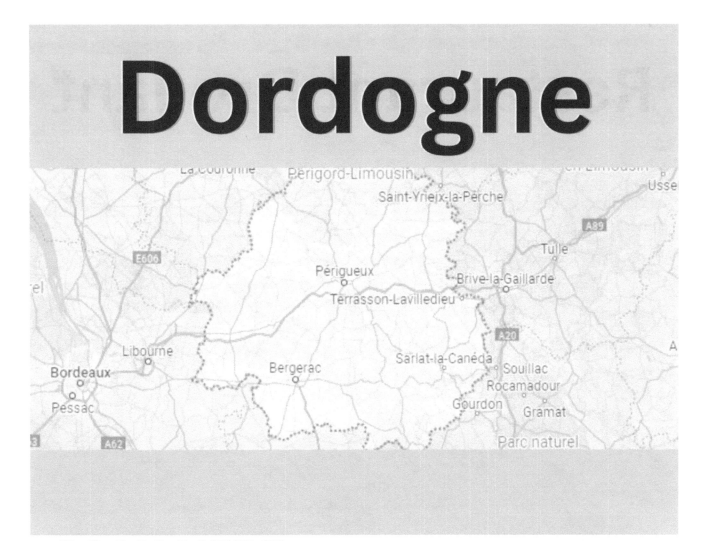

SCAN HERE

HOW TO USE QR CODE

- Open your phone's camera app or download scanner app from play store or apple store
- Point the camera at the QR code for a few seconds (no need to take a photo).
- A link should appear on the display, leading you to the location of the code

Restaurant Drouant

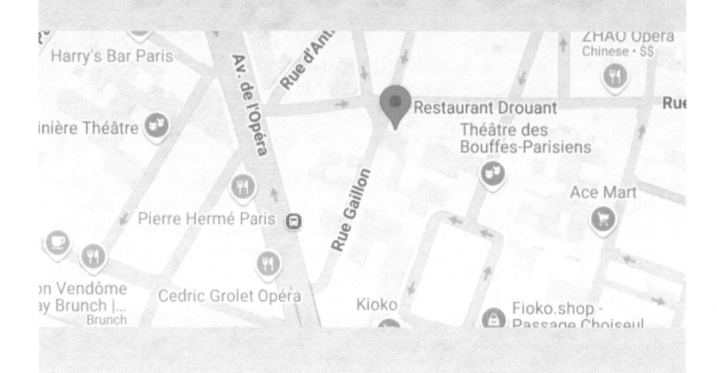

SCAN HERE

HOW TO USE QR CODE

- Open your phone's camera app or download scanner app from play store or apple store
- Point the camera at the QR code for a few seconds (no need to take a photo).
- A link should appear on the display, leading you to the location of the code

Normandy

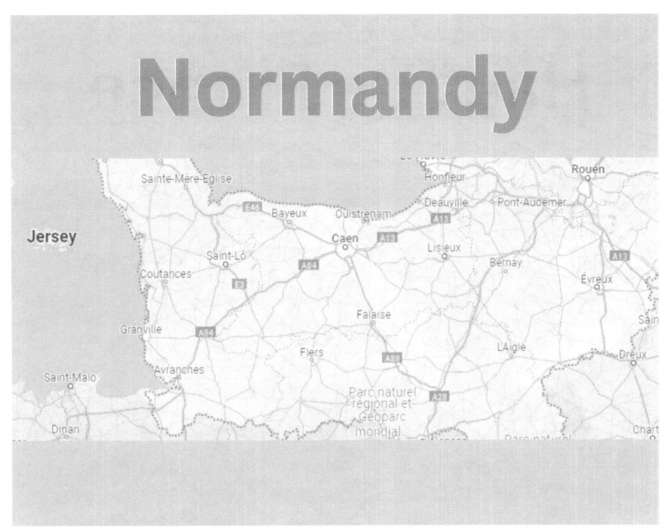

SCAN HERE

HOW TO USE QR CODE

- Open your phone's camera app or download scanner app from play store or apple store
- Point the camera at the QR code for a few seconds (no need to take a photo).
- A link should appear on the display, leading you to the location of the code

Haut de France

Haut de France

SCAN HERE

HOW TO USE QR CODE

- Open your phone's camera app or download scanner app from play store or apple store
- Point the camera at the QR code for a few seconds (no need to take a photo).
- A link should appear on the display, leading you to the location of the code

Loire Valley

SCAN HERE

HOW TO USE QR CODE

- Open your phone's camera app or download scanner app from play store or apple store
- Point the camera at the QR code for a few seconds (no need to take a photo).
- A link should appear on the display, leading you to the location of the code

French Riviera

SCAN HERE

HOW TO USE QR CODE

- Open your phone's camera app or download scanner app from play store or apple store
- Point the camera at the QR code for a few seconds (no need to take a photo).
- A link should appear on the display, leading you to the location of the code

Burgundy

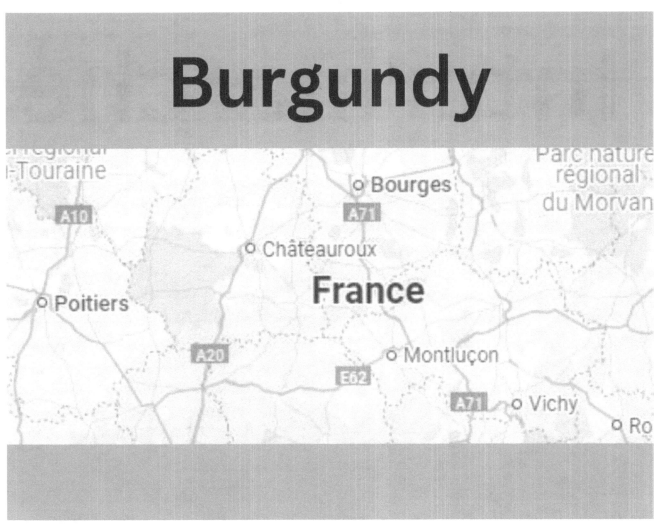

SCAN HERE

HOW TO USE QR CODE

- Open your phone's camera app or download scanner app from play store or apple store
- Point the camera at the QR code for a few seconds (no need to take a photo).
- A link should appear on the display, leading you to the location of the code

Intermarché

SCAN HERE

HOW TO USE QR CODE

- Open your phone's camera app or download scanner app from play store or apple store
- Point the camera at the QR code for a few seconds (no need to take a photo).
- A link should appear on the display, leading you to the location of the code

AIRE DE LA VENDÉE

SCAN HERE   HOW TO USE QR CODE

- Open your phone's camera app or download scanner app from play store or apple store
- Point the camera at the QR code for a few seconds (no need to take a photo).
- A link should appear on the display, leading you to the location of the code

Chapter 6

Hidden Gems of France

Off-the-Beaten-Path Destinations

France is internationally celebrated for its iconic sites, such as the Eiffel Tower, the lavender fields in Provence, and the châteaux of the Loire Valley. Yet, beyond these popular destinations, numerous hidden treasures truly exemplify the country's charm. These hidden gems offer travelers the chance to explore underrated villages, untouched forests, and serene coastal spots. From quirky museums to vibrant local festivals, these locations promise unique experiences that provide a deeper connection to France's rich heritage and natural beauty.

1. Underrated Villages

France is home to countless picturesque villages, each with its character and story. These lesser-visited locations often boast stunning architecture, breathtaking views, and warm, welcoming communities.

a. Collonges-la-Rouge (Corrèze, Nouvelle-Aquitaine)

Known as the "Red Village," Collonges-la-Rouge is a feast for the eyes with its deep-red sandstone buildings.

Highlights: Cobblestone streets, medieval towers, and local artisan shops.

Must-Try: Walnut-based delicacies and locally produced wines.

Why Visit? It's a member of Les plus Beaux Villages de France (The Most Beautiful Villages of France), but less crowded than others in the association.

b. Pérouges (Auvergne-Rhône-Alpes)

This medieval village near Lyon feels like stepping back in time.

Highlights: Stone buildings, ancient ramparts, and the village square.

Must-Try: The famous galette de Pérouges, a thin, sweet pastry.

Why Visit?: Its cinematic beauty has made it a filming location for historical movies.

2. Forest Retreats and Natural Escapes

While France is celebrated for its urban beauty, its forests and natural parks are equally enchanting, offering tranquility and outdoor adventures.

A. Forêt d'Orleans (Centre-Val de Loire)

The largest forest in France is a lush expanse perfect for hiking, birdwatching, and cycling.

Unique Features: A mix of oak, pine, and beech trees.

Activities: Explore historic hunting trails and spot deer or wild boar.

B. Fontainebleau Forest (Île-de-France)

Just an hour from Paris, this forest is famous for its bouldering opportunities and serene beauty.

Unique Features: Massive rock formations and royal hunting lodges.

Why Visit?: A favorite escape for Parisians looking to reconnect with nature.

3. Quirky Museums and Cultural Stops

For those who enjoy a dose of the unusual, France boasts a collection of quirky museums and cultural attractions that go beyond the Louvre and Musée d'Orsay.

a. The Museum of Vampires and Legendary Creatures (Paris)

A macabre yet fascinating museum dedicated to the folklore of vampires.

Why Visit?: It's an offbeat way to explore French and European legends.

b. The Museum of Automatons (La Rochelle)

This charming museum displays intricate, mechanical figurines from centuries past.

Why visit?: It's a whimsical stop for families and anyone intrigued by craftsmanship.

4. Local Celebrations and Festivals

The vibrant lineup of festivals in France highlights regional customs and a sense of community.

a. Menton Lemon Festival (Fête du Citron, Provence-Alpes-Côte d'Azur)

Held every February, this festival celebrates citrus fruits with parades, sculptures, and exhibitions.

Why Visit?: It's a colorful and fragrant spectacle.

b. The Giant Omelette Festival (Bessières, Occitanie)

This annual event features the preparation of a massive omelet using thousands of eggs.

Why Visit?: It's a fun and quirky celebration of local culinary traditions.

Why Explore Hidden Gems?

Venturing beyond the beaten path allows you to uncover France's quieter, more authentic side. These destinations provide a chance to connect with locals, experience unique traditions, and enjoy natural beauty away from crowds. Whether you're strolling through a red-hued village, hiking in a tranquil forest, or attending a quirky festival, these hidden gems ensure a memorable and enriching travel experience.

Natural Wonders

France's stunning natural scenery is one of its most overlooked gems. From the turquoise waters of dramatic canyons to sprawling wetlands teeming with wildlife and the majestic peaks of the Pyrenees, these natural wonders provide unparalleled opportunities for exploration. Whether you're an avid hiker or a road-tripper seeking scenic stops, these destinations promise awe-inspiring experiences.

1. Gorges du Verdon (Provence-Alpes-Côte d'Azur)

Often referred to as the "Grand Canyon of Europe," the Gorges du Verdon is a spectacular river canyon carved by the Verdon River.

Highlights

Dramatic Cliffs: Towering limestone walls rise as high as 700 meters, creating jaw-dropping vistas.

Road Trip Tip: Drive along the Corniche Sublime for panoramic views of the canyon's most dramatic points.

Activities

Hiking trails like the Sentier Blanc-Martel, which offers stunning views and access to hidden riverbanks.

Boat rentals for an up-close exploration of the canyon.

Why Visit?: This is an ideal spot for thrill-seekers and photographers, offering a combination of striking landscapes and peaceful waters.

2. Camargue Wetlands (Provence-Alpes-Côte d'Azur)

The Camargue is a unique ecosystem created where the Rhône River meets the Mediterranean Sea. Famed for its wild allure and varied wildlife, it serves as a haven for outdoor enthusiasts.

Highlights:

Wildlife: Spot pink flamingos, wild white horses, and black bulls in their natural habitat.

Salt Flats: The Salin de Giraud salt flats glisten in shades of pink under the sun.

Activities

Take a scenic drive to discover hidden lagoons and small fishing villages.

Horseback riding tours offer an authentic way to explore the wetlands.

Why Visit?: The blend of striking landscapes and rare wildlife makes the Camargue an unforgettable destination.

3. Best Hiking Trails Accessible by Car

France's hiking trails cater to all levels, offering breathtaking views and access to secluded natural wonders.

a. The Sentier des Ocres (Roussillon, Provence)

Why it's Special: A short, easy hike through ochre cliffs and vibrant red canyons.

Access Tip: Nearby parking lots make it an easy stop on a Provence road trip.

b. GR20 (Corsica)

Why It's Special: Known as one of Europe's toughest trails, it offers rugged beauty and panoramic island views.

Access Tip: Park in small villages like Calenzana to begin a day hike instead of the full trek.

Cultural Experiences

France's appeal comes not just from its magnificent scenery but also from its vibrant local culture. Exploring artisan workshops, bustling markets, and unique traditions is a window into the country's soul.

1. Artisan Workshops

a. Pottery in Saint-Amand-en-Puisaye (Burgundy)

What to Expect: Visit studios and learn the art of traditional French pottery-making.

Why Visit?: This village embodies the core of Burgundy's ceramic heritage.

b. Knife-Making in Laguiole (Occitanie)

What to Expect: Discover workshops specializing in the production of Laguiole knives, famous for their outstanding craftsmanship.

Why Visit?: These knives serve as both artistic masterpieces and symbols of French tradition.

2. Local Markets

France's markets are more than just places to shop they're vibrant community hubs that reflect the flavors and traditions of the region.

a. Marché des Lices (Rennes, Brittany)

Why it's Special: One of France's largest markets, offering everything from fresh seafood to regional pastries like kouign-amann.

b. Cours Saleya Market (Nice, Côte d'Azur)

Why It's Special: A colorful flower and food market set against the backdrop of the Mediterranean.

3. Unique Traditions

a. Transhumance Festivals (Provence and Pyrenees)

What It Is: A celebration of moving livestock to higher pastures, complete with parades and local feasts.

Why It's Special: It's a glimpse into the agricultural roots of rural France.

b. Wine Harvest Festivals (Various Regions)

What It Is: Celebrate the grape harvest with wine tastings, music, and local dishes.

Why it's Special: a festive way to connect with France's winemaking heritage.

Why These Experiences Matter

France's natural wonders and cultural traditions reveal a side of the country that's both authentic and enriching. Whether you're marveling at dramatic landscapes or immersing yourself in artisanal crafts, these experiences add depth to your journey

Eiffel Tower

SCAN HERE

HOW TO USE QR CODE

- Open your phone's camera app or download scanner app from play store or apple store
- Point the camera at the QR code for a few seconds (no need to take a photo).
- A link should appear on the display, leading you to the location of the code

Loire Valley

SCAN HERE

HOW TO USE QR CODE

- Open your phone's camera app or download scanner app from play store or apple store
- Point the camera at the QR code for a few seconds (no need to take a photo).
- A link should appear on the display, leading you to the location of the code

Collonges-la-Rouge

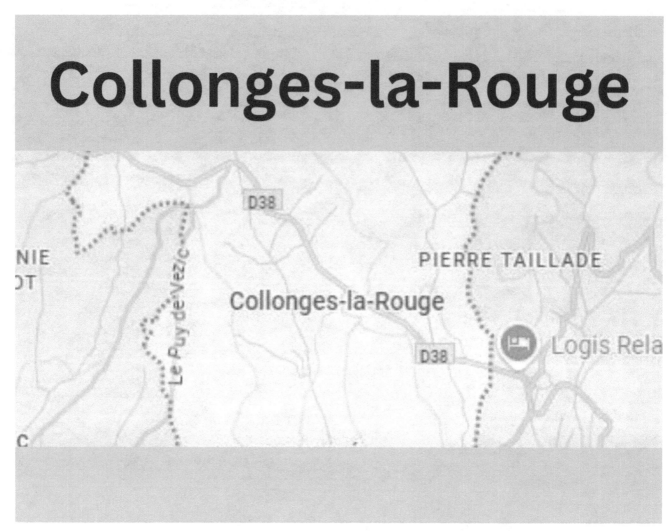

SCAN HERE

HOW TO USE QR CODE

- Open your phone's camera app or download scanner app from play store or apple store
- Point the camera at the QR code for a few seconds (no need to take a photo).
- A link should appear on the display, leading you to the location of the code

Pérouges

SCAN HERE

HOW TO USE QR CODE

- Open your phone's camera app or download scanner app from play store or apple store
- Point the camera at the QR code for a few seconds (no need to take a photo).
- A link should appear on the display, leading you to the location of the code

Forest of Fontainebleau

SCAN HERE

HOW TO USE QR CODE

- Open your phone's camera app or download scanner app from play store or apple store
- Point the camera at the QR code for a few seconds (no need to take a photo).
- A link should appear on the display, leading you to the location of the code

Louvre Museum

Pyramide du Louvre
Iconic glass pyramid
leading to museum

us les traits
rtius (copie)

Musée du Louvre

Louvre -

Cour Carrée

Mona Lisa)

Saint-Germa
Gra

Quai Franço

Jardin de
l'Infante

SCAN HERE

HOW TO USE QR CODE

- Open your phone's camera app or download scanner app from play store or apple store
- Point the camera at the QR code for a few seconds (no need to take a photo).
- A link should appear on the display, leading you to the location of the code

Musée d'Orsay

SCAN HERE

HOW TO USE QR CODE

- Open your phone's camera app or download scanner app from play store or apple store
- Point the camera at the QR code for a few seconds (no need to take a photo).
- A link should appear on the display, leading you to the location of the code

La Rochelle

SCAN HERE

HOW TO USE QR CODE

- Open your phone's camera app or download scanner app from play store or apple store
- Point the camera at the QR code for a few seconds (no need to take a photo).
- A link should appear on the display, leading you to the location of the code

Verdon Gorge

regional
du Verdon

D952

La Palud-sur-Verdon

Point de vue   D952   BOULOGNE

SCAN HERE   HOW TO USE QR CODE

- Open your phone's camera app or download scanner app from play store or apple store
- Point the camera at the QR code for a few seconds (no need to take a photo).
- A link should appear on the display, leading you to the location of the code

Camargue

SCAN HERE   HOW TO USE QR CODE

- Open your phone's camera app or download scanner app from play store or apple store
- Point the camera at the QR code for a few seconds (no need to take a photo).
- A link should appear on the display, leading you to the location of the code

Salin-de-Giraud

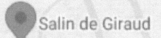

SCAN HERE   HOW TO USE QR CODE

- Open your phone's camera app or download scanner app from play store or apple store
- Point the camera at the QR code for a few seconds (no need to take a photo).
- A link should appear on the display, leading you to the location of the code

Le Sentier des Ocres

SCAN HERE

HOW TO USE QR CODE

- Open your phone's camera app or download scanner app from play store or apple store
- Point the camera at the QR code for a few seconds (no need to take a photo).
- A link should appear on the display, leading you to the location of the code

Saint-Amand-en-Puisaye

Maison de Santé
Amandinoise

Centre Social et
de Puisaye

Franc
Saint-Amar

nm vert
len center

D955

Saint-Amand-en-Puisaye

Mairie de
Saint-Amand-en-Puisaye

St amand en puisaye

SCAN HERE

HOW TO USE QR CODE

- Open your phone's camera app or download scanner app from play store or apple store
- Point the camera at the QR code for a few seconds (no need to take a photo).
- A link should appear on the display, leading you to the location of the code

Laguiole

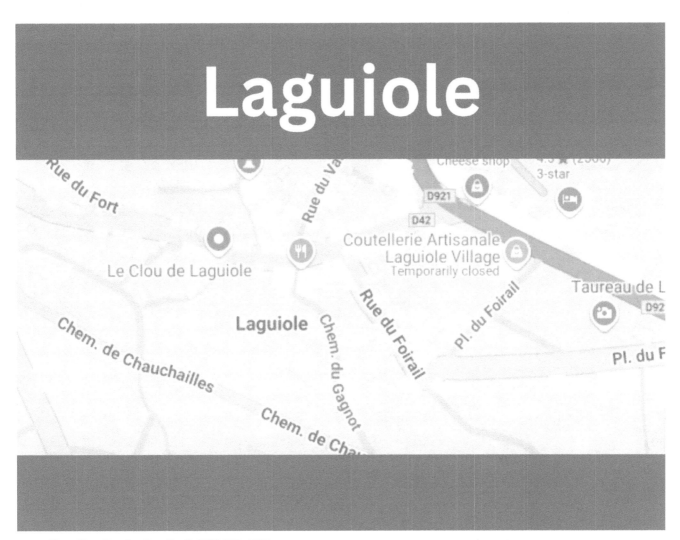

SCAN HERE

HOW TO USE QR CODE

- Open your phone's camera app or download scanner app from play store or apple store
- Point the camera at the QR code for a few seconds (no need to take a photo).
- A link should appear on the display, leading you to the location of the code

Marché des Lices

SCAN HERE   HOW TO USE QR CODE

- Open your phone's camera app or download scanner app from play store or apple store
- Point the camera at the QR code for a few seconds (no need to take a photo).
- A link should appear on the display, leading you to the location of the code

Marché Aux Fleurs - Cours Saleya - Nice

SCAN HERE

HOW TO USE QR CODE

- Open your phone's camera app or download scanner app from play store or apple store
- Point the camera at the QR code for a few seconds (no need to take a photo).
- A link should appear on the display, leading you to the location of the code

Provence

SCAN HERE

HOW TO USE QR CODE

- Open your phone's camera app or download scanner app from play store or apple store
- Point the camera at the QR code for a few seconds (no need to take a photo).
- A link should appear on the display, leading you to the location of the code

Pyrenees

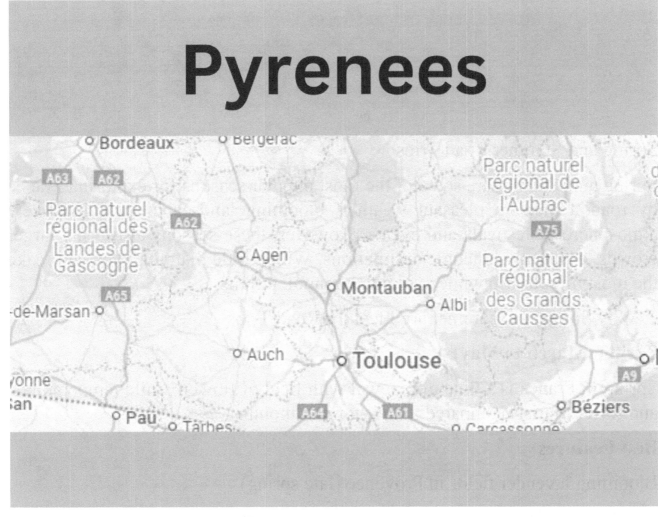

SCAN HERE HOW TO USE QR CODE

- Open your phone's camera app or download scanner app from play store or apple store
- Point the camera at the QR code for a few seconds (no need to take a photo).
- A link should appear on the display, leading you to the location of the code

Chapter 7

Spring and Summer Road Trips

Spring and summer are some of the most popular seasons for exploring France by road, thanks to pleasant weather, blooming landscapes, and the lively atmosphere of festivals and events. However, these seasons also bring larger crowds, especially to iconic destinations. With a little planning, you can make the most of your trip while avoiding common pitfalls.

1. Why Spring and summer are Ideal for Road Trips

Spring (March to May)

Spring in France is a time of renewal with field of flowers, mild temperatures, and fewer tourists compared to the summer months.

Best Features

Blooming lavender fields in Provence (late spring)

Comfortable driving conditions with less congestion on the roads.

Summer (June to August)

Summer brings longer days, warm sunshine, and bustling energy to French towns and countryside alike.

Best Features:

Coastal regions like the Côte d'Azur are alive with vibrant activity.

Lively festivals, including Bastille Day celebrations (July 14).

Access to high-altitude destinations like the Alps or Pyrenees, perfect for escaping the heat.

2. Peak Tourist Destinations for spring and summer

While some destinations attract tourists year-round, others shine particularly bright during these warmer months. Below are some top spots to include in your road trip itinerary, along with insider tips to beat the crowds.

a. Provence in spring

Highlights

Lavender fields at their peak bloom from mid-June to mid-July (plan early summer visits for this).

Almond trees and cherry blossoms herald the beginning of spring.

Quaint markets sell fresh produce, herbs, and flowers.

Tips

Visit smaller villages like Roussillon and Gordes early in the day to avoid tour groups.

Use regional roads instead of main highways to enjoy scenic landscapes.

b. Paris in summer

Highlights

Iconic landmarks such as the Eiffel Tower, the Seine River, and the Gardens of Versailles are bustling with activity.

Open-air cinemas, music festivals, and riverside pop-up cafes.

Tips

Purchase tickets to major attractions in advance and aim for early morning or late evening visits to skip long lines.

Take a leisurely bike ride instead of driving in the city; Paris is especially cycle-friendly during summer.

3. Avoiding Crowds in High-Season Destinations

Crowds can diminish the magic of exploring France during its busiest times. However, with a few strategic adjustments, you can enjoy popular attractions without feeling overwhelmed.

Travel during Shoulder Times

In spring, plan your visit for late March or April to enjoy the blooming landscapes before the summer rush.

In summer, aim for late June or early September, when children are still in school and the weather is warm.

Off-the-Beaten-Path Alternatives

Instead of Mont Saint-Michel, visit the less crowded Abbaye de Jumièges in Normandy.

Skip the beaches of Saint-Tropez for the peaceful Calanques National Park near Marseille.

Early Starts and Late Nights

Begin your sightseeing early in the morning to enjoy a few hours before crowds arrive.

Alternatively, explore iconic spots in the evening when tour buses and day-trippers have left.

4. Road Trip Essentials for spring and summer

Proper preparation can make your journey smoother and more enjoyable during these busy seasons.

a. Plan for the Heat (Summer)

Pack Essentials: Sunblock, hats, reusable water bottles, and cooling towels are crucial for staying comfortable during summer.

Car Maintenance: Ensure your vehicle's air conditioning is in working order and check tire pressure before embarking on long drives.

b. Prepare for Changing Weather (spring)

Pack Layers: While spring days are pleasant, mornings and evenings can be chilly, especially in mountainous regions.

Rain Gear: Keep an umbrella or lightweight rain jacket handy for unexpected showers.

5. Must-Have Apps and Tools for Peak Travel Seasons

a. Parking Apps

Apps like Park4Night help you locate parking spots or rest areas, especially near busy attractions.

b. Real-Time Traffic Updates

Use apps such as Waze or Google Maps to anticipate traffic congestion and find alternate routes.

c. Weather Apps

Install apps like Météo-France for reliable forecasts to help plan your day's activities.

Why spring and Summer Road Trips Are Worth It

Despite the challenges of busier roads and bustling destinations, spring and summer road trips in France allow travelers to experience the country at its vibrant best. From verdant vineyards and flower-strewn villages to sun-soaked coastlines and mountain vistas, this is when France truly comes alive. With thoughtful planning and flexibility, you can craft a memorable journey filled with scenic beauty, cultural richness, and authentic encounters.

Fall and Winter Adventures

Scenic Autumn Drives and Top Ski Resorts

While spring and summer are popular times for exploring France, fall and winter offer their own unique appeal, transforming the country into a picturesque wonderland of golden hues, festive charm, and snow-dusted peaks. Whether you're drawn to the fiery colors of autumn or the pristine beauty of winter landscapes, these seasons present opportunities for unforgettable road trips.

1. Fall: A Palette of Gold, Orange, and Red

Why fall is Ideal for Road Trips

Fall in France (September to November) is synonymous with cooler temperatures, quieter roads, and stunning natural scenery. From wine harvests to golden forests, this season is perfect for travelers seeking a more peaceful journey.

Scenic Autumn Drives

a. Alsace Wine Route

Highlights

Vibrant vineyards stretch as far as the eye can see, their leaves turning shades of red, orange, and gold.

Charming villages like Riquewihr and Obernai with their half-timbered houses and cobblestone streets.

Seasonal wine festivals mark the end of the grape harvest.

Driving Tip

Take your time to explore local wineries, but always ensure you have a designated driver or use local transport options for wine tastings.

b. Dordogne Valley

Highlights

Tree-lined roads adorned with fiery autumn leaves.

Castles like Château de Beynac and prehistoric caves offer a mix of history and natural beauty.

Peaceful riverside villages such as La Roque-Gageac and Domme.

Driving Tip

Early mornings provide a magical atmosphere with mist rising from the rivers.

2. Winter: A Season of Snow and Festivity

Why winter is Ideal for Road Trips

Winter (December to February) transforms France into a land of contrasts. Coastal regions remain mild and welcoming, while mountain ranges and ski resorts provide the quintessential winter experience.

Top Winter Destinations for Road Trippers

a. French Alps: Skiing and Snowy Splendor

Highlights

Well-known ski destinations like Chamonix and Les Deux Alpes serve skiers of all abilities.

Snow-covered mountain villages offer cozy chalets and roaring fireplaces.

Non-skiers can enjoy winter hiking, snowshoeing, or relaxing at luxurious alpine spas.

Driving Tip

Equip your car with winter tires or snow chains, especially in mountain regions where snowfalls can be heavy..

b. Normandy and Brittany's Coastal Charm

Highlights

Mild winters and fewer tourists make these regions a peaceful retreat.

Rugged coastlines, historic landmarks like Mont Saint-Michel, and seafood feasts are key attractions.

Winter storms bring dramatic waves, offering spectacular views for photographers and nature enthusiasts.

Driving Tip

Coastal roads can be slick from rain or sea spray—maintain a safe distance from other vehicles.

3. Seasonal Activities and Festive Highlights

Autumn Events

Wine Harvest Festivals

Participate in local celebrations, such as the Fête des Vendanges in Montmartre, Paris, or in small villages across Burgundy and Bordeaux.

Chestnut Festivals

Especially popular in regions like Ardèche, these festivals showcase roasted chestnuts, chestnut-based dishes, and local traditions.

Winter Activities

Christmas Markets

Strasbourg's Christkindelsmärik is among the oldest and most famous, while smaller markets in Provence and the Loire Valley offer more intimate experiences.

Ski and Snowboarding:

France boasts some of the best ski resorts in Europe, with slopes for everyone from beginners to experts.

Carnival in Nice

This February event features parades, flower battles, and lively celebrations against the backdrop of the Côte d'Azur.

4. Why Fall and Winter Road Trips Are Worth the Journey

Exploring France in fall and winter provides a unique perspective on the country's beauty and culture. The quieter atmosphere allows travelers to immerse themselves in local life, while the changing landscapes offer a feast for the eyes. Whether you're admiring the fiery colors of autumn vineyards or enjoying the festive glow of winter markets, these seasons bring a sense of magic to every mile you travel.

Weather Considerations Preparing for Changing Conditions across France

France's diverse geography creates varying weather patterns across its regions, making it essential for road trippers to plan for shifting conditions throughout their journey. From the temperate coastal areas of Brittany to the snowy peaks of the French Alps, understanding the seasonal climate will ensure a smoother and safer experience.

1. Overview of France's Climate Zones

a. Coastal Climates

Regions: Brittany, Normandy, and the Côte d'Azur.

Characteristics

Mild winters with occasional rain.

Cool breezes in spring and summer, with warmer, sunny days along the Mediterranean.

What to Expect

In the north (Brittany and Normandy), be prepared for sudden showers, even in summer.

In the south, winter remains relatively mild, though evenings can be chilly.

b. Mountain Climates

Regions: Alps, Pyrenees, and Massif Central.

Characteristics

Harsh winters with significant snowfall, especially from November to March.

Mild, pleasant summers that are perfect for hiking.

What to Expect

Sudden temperature drops, even in summer.

Heavy snow and ice in winter require specialized driving gear and skills.

2. Seasonal Weather Considerations

Spring (March-May)

Weather Patterns

Changeable weather that includes a blend of sunshine, rainfall, and occasional cool breezes.

Tips for Travelers

Pack layers, including a light rain jacket.

Be cautious of slick roads after spring rains, especially in rural areas.

Summer (June-August)

Weather Patterns:

The southern regions are characterized by heat and dryness, whereas central and northern areas see sporadic thunderstorms.

Tips for Travelers:

Carry plenty of water to stay hydrated during heatwaves.

Avoid driving during peak afternoon heat in southern France to prevent overheating vehicles.

Autumn (September-November)

Weather Patterns

Cool mornings and evenings, with vibrant fall foliage dominating the countryside.

Tips for Travelers

Keep an umbrella handy for unexpected rain showers.

Beware of foggy conditions in the early mornings, especially in the Dordogne and Loire Valley.

Winter (December-February)

Weather Patterns:

Snow and ice in mountain regions, while coastal and inland areas remain cool and damp.

Tips for Travelers:

Equip your car with snow tires or chains when traveling to the Alps or Pyrenees.

Watch for black ice on roads, especially in early mornings or in shaded areas.

3. Preparing for Weather-Related Challenges

Rain and Slick Roads

Common Regions: Northern France, Brittany, and Normandy.

Precautions

Reduce speed during rain to maintain control.

Ensure windshield wipers are in good condition for clear visibility.

Snow and Ice

Common Regions: Alps, Pyrenees, and occasionally in inland regions during cold spells.

Precautions

Keep snow chains readily available and know how to attach them.

Use low gears on icy or snowy descents to maintain control.

Fog

Common Regions: Loire Valley, Dordogne, and Burgundy.

Precautions

Use fog lights where permitted and avoid high beams.

Reduce your speed and maintain a larger space between vehicles.

Strong Winds

Common Regions: Provence (mistral winds) and coastal areas.

Precautions:

Firmly grip the steering wheel to maintain control.

Be careful when passing large vehicles or navigating through open areas.

4. Weather Apps and Tools for Travelers

Météo-France: The national weather service app, provides detailed and reliable forecasts.

AccuWeather: Offers long-range forecasts and real-time weather alerts.

Waze and Google Maps: Include weather-related road condition updates, such as closures or delays.

Local Radio Stations: Often provide up-to-date weather and traffic reports for specific regions.

5. Adapting to Weather on the Road

Stay Flexible

Weather can change swiftly, especially in mountainous or coastal regions. Always be prepared to adjust your itinerary, whether it means delaying a drive due to fog or rerouting to avoid flooded roads.

Check Local Weather Updates

Before heading out each day, review the weather forecast for your destination and along your route. Being knowledgeable allows you to predict and prepare for potential difficulties.

Embrace the Experience

Rainy days offer cozy moments in cafés or opportunities to explore museums. Snowy landscapes in the Alps or frosty vineyards in Burgundy create breathtaking scenery. Instead of letting the weather dictate your trip, let it enhance your adventure.

By understanding France's varied climates and preparing for potential weather shifts, you'll be equipped to handle any conditions with ease. From sunny Mediterranean drives to snowy alpine adventures, France's beauty shines in every season making the journey as memorable as the destination themselves.

Provence-Alpes-Côte d'Azur

SCAN HERE

HOW TO USE QR CODE

- Open your phone's camera app or download scanner app from play store or apple store
- Point the camera at the QR code for a few seconds (no need to take a photo).
- A link should appear on the display, leading you to the location of the code

Paris

SCAN HERE

HOW TO USE QR CODE

- Open your phone's camera app or download scanner app from play store or apple store
- Point the camera at the QR code for a few seconds (no need to take a photo).
- A link should appear on the display, leading you to the location of the code

Eiffel Tower

SCAN HERE

HOW TO USE QR CODE

- Open your phone's camera app or download scanner app from play store or apple store
- Point the camera at the QR code for a few seconds (no need to take a photo).
- A link should appear on the display, leading you to the location of the code

Seine

SCAN HERE

HOW TO USE QR CODE

- Open your phone's camera app or download scanner app from play store or apple store
- Point the camera at the QR code for a few seconds (no need to take a photo).
- A link should appear on the display, leading you to the location of the code

Abbaye de Jumièges

Auberge des Ruines
French

D143

L'heure des thés

Abbaye de Jumièges

SCAN HERE   HOW TO USE QR CODE

- Open your phone's camera app or download scanner app from play store or apple store
- Point the camera at the QR code for a few seconds (no need to take a photo).
- A link should appear on the display, leading you to the location of the code

Parc national des Calanques

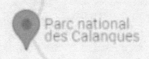

SCAN HERE

HOW TO USE QR CODE

- Open your phone's camera app or download scanner app from play store or apple store
- Point the camera at the QR code for a few seconds (no need to take a photo).
- A link should appear on the display, leading you to the location of the code

Riquewihr

Jardins des Papillons
Temporarily closed

Hunawihr

D1B

SCAN HERE   HOW TO USE QR CODE

- Open your phone's camera app or download scanner app from play store or apple store
- Point the camera at the QR code for a few seconds (no need to take a photo).
- A link should appear on the display, leading you to the location of the code

Château de Beynac

SCAN HERE

HOW TO USE QR CODE

- Open your phone's camera app or download scanner app from play store or apple store
- Point the camera at the QR code for a few seconds (no need to take a photo).
- A link should appear on the display, leading you to the location of the code

Chamonix

SCAN HERE

HOW TO USE QR CODE

- Open your phone's camera app or download scanner app from play store or apple store
- Point the camera at the QR code for a few seconds (no need to take a photo).
- A link should appear on the display, leading you to the location of the code

Mont Saint-Michel

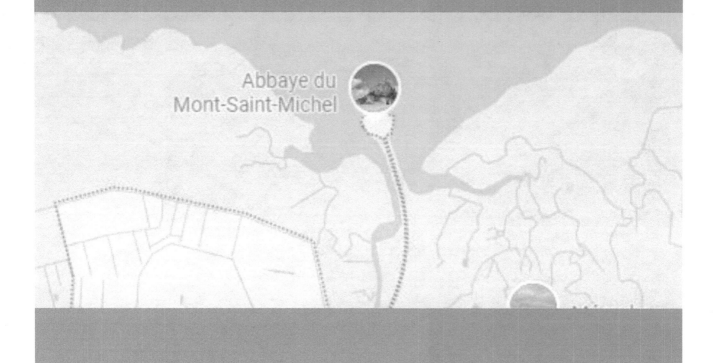

SCAN HERE

HOW TO USE QR CODE

- Open your phone's camera app or download scanner app from play store or apple store
- Point the camera at the QR code for a few seconds (no need to take a photo).
- A link should appear on the display, leading you to the location of the code

Christmas market

SCAN HERE

HOW TO USE QR CODE

- Open your phone's camera app or download scanner app from play store or apple store
- Point the camera at the QR code for a few seconds (no need to take a photo).
- A link should appear on the display, leading you to the location of the code

Nice

SCAN HERE

HOW TO USE QR CODE

- Open your phone's camera app or download scanner app from play store or apple store
- Point the camera at the QR code for a few seconds (no need to take a photo).
- A link should appear on the display, leading you to the location of the code

Brittany

SCAN HERE

HOW TO USE QR CODE

- Open your phone's camera app or download scanner app from play store or apple store
- Point the camera at the QR code for a few seconds (no need to take a photo).
- A link should appear on the display, leading you to the location of the code

Normandy

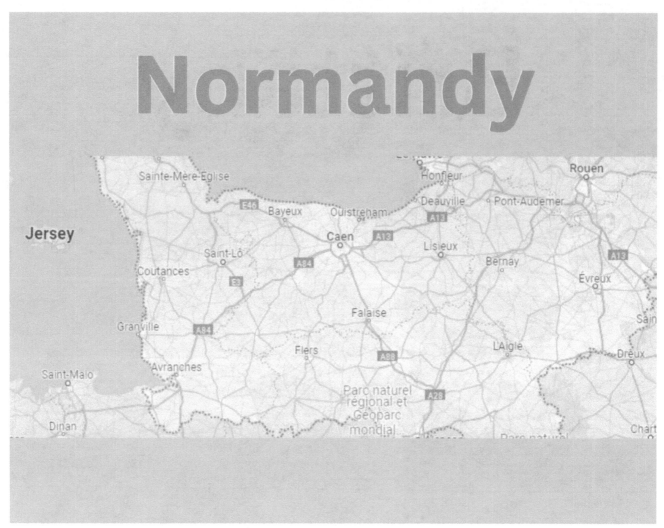

SCAN HERE

HOW TO USE QR CODE

- Open your phone's camera app or download scanner app from play store or apple store
- Point the camera at the QR code for a few seconds (no need to take a photo).
- A link should appear on the display, leading you to the location of the code

Pyrenees

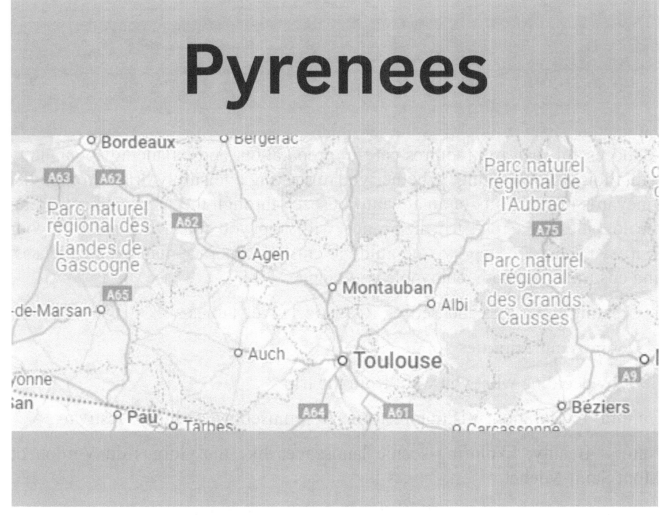

SCAN HERE

HOW TO USE QR CODE

- Open your phone's camera app or download scanner app from play store or apple store
- Point the camera at the QR code for a few seconds (no need to take a photo).
- A link should appear on the display, leading you to the location of the code

Chapter 8

Planning Your Perfect Road Trip

A successful road trip requires careful preparation, and balancing spontaneity with thoughtful planning. Whether you're seeking a leisurely drive through the vineyards of Bordeaux or an adventurous trek through the Alps, understanding the logistics of a road trip in France will help you make the most of your journey. These are step-by-step guide to crafting itinerary managing expenses, and ensuring a smooth, enjoyable experience.

1. Creating Itineraries and Setting Realistic Travel Times

a. Define Your Priorities

Start by deciding what you want from the trip

Cultural Exploration: Visiting historic sites, museums, and local festivals.

Natural Beauty: Exploring scenic landscapes like the Gorges du Verdon or Mont Saint-Michel.

Culinary Adventures: Sampling regional delicacies and wines.

b. Break down the Journey

Choose Key Destinations: Pick 3–5 must-visit locations to form the backbone of your trip.

Example: Paris → Loire Valley → Dordogne → Provence.

Map out Distances: Use tools like Google Maps or Michelin Route Planner to calculate travel times.

Keep daily drives under 3–4 hours to avoid fatigue.

Plan Stopovers: Identify towns or landmarks en route where you can take breaks or explore.

c. Sample 6-Day Itinerary

Day 1-2: Paris and Versailles.

Day 3: Loire Valley châteaux.

Day 4: Drive to Dordogne, stopping in Limoges.

Day 5: Explore Sarlat-la-Canéda and prehistoric caves.

Day 6: End with a scenic drive along the Côte d'Azur.

2. Budgeting for Tolls, Fuel, and Accommodations

a. Estimating Tolls

France's autoroutes (highways) are often tolled, especially on major routes:

Cost: €10–€60 depending on the distance.

How to Pay

Cash or cards at toll booths.

Prépayé badges like Liber-t for convenience.

Tip: Use toll calculators, such as the one on the official Autoroutes.fr site, to estimate costs.

b. Managing Fuel Costs

Types of Fuel

Diesel (gazelle): Common and cheaper than petrol (essence).

Petrol: Available as SP95 or SP98.

Average Costs:

Diesel: ~€1.70 per liter.

Petrol: ~€1.90 per liter.

Saving Tips

Fill up at supermarkets (e.g., Carrefour, Leclerc) instead of highway stations.

Use apps like Essence&Co to locate the cheapest fuel nearby.

c. Booking Accommodations

Types of Lodging:

Budget-friendly: Chain hotels like Ibis Budget or B&B Hotels.

Mid-range: Charming guesthouses (chambres d'hôtes) or boutique hotels.

Luxury: High-end stays in castles or Michelin-starred hotel restaurants.

Costs:

Budget: €50–€80 per night.

Mid-range: €100–€200 per night.

Luxury: €300+ per night.

3. Practical Planning Tips

a. Assemble Your Documents

Driver's License: Ensure you meet French requirements, and carry an IDP if necessary.

Insurance: Verify coverage for car rentals and road trips abroad.

Car Rental Agreement: Double-check terms, particularly for mileage limits or cross-border travel.

b. Pack Wisely

Car Essentials:

Emergency kit (reflective vests, warning triangle, spare tire).

Universal GPS or smartphone holder.

Personal Items:

Lightweight clothing for summer or layers for winter.

Comfortable shoes for walking tours or hikes.

c. Leverage Travel Apps

ViaMichelin: For detailed maps, toll costs, and route options.

Park4Night: Perfect for campers and caravanners looking for overnight parking spots.

The Fork: Find and book restaurants with real-time reviews and deals.

4. Final Checklist for a Stress-Free Road Trip

Before Departure:

Check your car's condition (tires, oil, fluids).

Save offline maps to be ready for areas with poor network coverage.

En Route:

Stop every 2–3 hours for breaks to stay alert.

Take advantage of scenic rest areas for picnics or quick sightseeing.

At Your Destination:

Get to know the local parking and traffic rules to prevent receiving any fines.

A well-planned road trip allows you to experience the best of France's cultural and natural treasures while minimizing stress and maximizing enjoyment. Whether cruising along the lavender-lined roads of Provence or traversing the rugged terrain of the Alps, careful preparation ensures that every moment is memorable. Follow this step-by-step guide to design an itinerary that reflects your interests, stays within your budget, and lets you fully embrace the freedom of the open road.

Essential steps for crafting a well-rounded road trip itinerary

Road trips offer an unparalleled way to explore France, allowing travelers to dive deep into its landscapes, history, and cuisine. Whether you're meandering through vineyard-laden hills, driving along the glittering Mediterranean coast, or exploring storybook villages in Alsace, proper planning ensures a seamless and enjoyable adventure.

Step 1: Creating Itineraries and Setting Realistic Travel Times

a. Understand Your Travel Goals

Your road trip should align with what excites you most about France. Ask yourself

Are you a history buff wanting to explore medieval towns and ancient ruins?

Is food your passion, driving you to sample fine wines and regional specialties?

Are you an outdoor enthusiast looking for breathtaking hikes and coastal vistas?

Once you've defined your priorities, selecting destinations becomes much easier.

b. Calculate Driving Times Accurately

Use Reliable Tools: Apps like Google Maps, ViaMichelin, or Waze provide accurate estimates but always add 15–20% more time for breaks, traffic, or sightseeing.

Adjust for Regional Roads: While highways (autoroutes) are fast, rural roads in regions like Dordogne or Brittany may be narrow and slower.

c. Keep Daily Drives Short and Enjoyable

Aim for 3–4 hours of driving per day to leave room for exploration.

Incorporate rest stops every 2 hours. France has excellent aire de repos (rest areas) with picnic spots, bathrooms, and sometimes even scenic viewpoints.

d. Example 7-Day Itinerary

For inspiration, here's a week-long road trip

Day 1-2: Arrive in Paris, explore the city, and visit Versailles.

Day 3: Drive to Normandy for the D-Day beaches and Mont Saint-Michel.

Day 4: Travel to the Loire Valley, stopping to explore its stunning châteaux.

Day 5: Head south to Dordogne, visiting medieval towns like Sarlat-la-Canéda.

Day 6: Explore the vineyards of Bordeaux and enjoy wine tastings.

Day 7: Drive to Provence to end with lavender fields and Roman ruins.

Step 8: Budgeting for Tolls, Fuel, and Accommodations

a. Estimating Costs for Tolls

France's extensive autoroute network often includes toll roads, which offer faster and more direct routes but come with costs.

Toll Costs

Average: €5–€10 per 100 km (~60 miles).

A Paris-to-Marseille drive (750 km) costs ~€60 in tolls.

Payment Methods

Cash or credit/debit cards at toll booths.

Prepaid passes like Liber-t offer contactless convenience and discounts.

Alternatives

Tip: Check toll calculators on apps like ViaMichelin to estimate your route's toll costs.

b. Fuel Costs and Savings Tips

Types of Fuel

Diesel (gazelle) is more common and cheaper than petrol (essence).

Petrol options: SP95 and SP98 (similar to regular and premium).

Average Prices

Diesel: €1.70 per liter (€6.40 per gallon).

Petrol: €1.90 per liter (€7.20 per gallon).

How to Save on Fuel

Fill up at supermarket stations like Carrefour or Leclerc instead of highway services.

Use apps like Essence&Co to find the cheapest fuel nearby.

Example Calculation

A 1,000 km (620 miles) trip in a diesel car averaging 5 liters per 100 km (~47 mpg) will cost ~€85 for fuel.

c. Budgeting for Accommodations

Types of Lodging

Budget: Chain hotels like Ibis Budget, Campanile, or Premiere Classe (€50–€80 per night).

Mid-Range: Charming guesthouses or boutique hotels (€90–€150 per night).

Luxury: High-end hotels, château stays, or Michelin-starred lodgings (€300+ per night).

Saving Tips

Look for off-season discounts (autumn and winter offer lower prices).

Use booking platforms like Booking.com or Airbnb for deals.

Careful planning turns a road trip into an enjoyable and worry-free experience. By mapping out realistic routes, accounting for expenses, and leaving room for flexibility, you can focus on enjoying the stunning sights and rich experiences that France offers. With the right preparation, your road trip will be filled with unforgettable memories, whether you're savoring local cuisine, marveling at breathtaking scenery, or delving into the country's storied history.

Packing Essentials for the Road

Starting a road trip in France assures breathtaking sights, tasty cuisine, and a range of landscapes. However, the success of your journey depends greatly on your preparation—particularly what you pack. Ensuring you have the right items for comfort, safety, and convenience can save you from unnecessary stress and enhance your travel experience. These are the outlines of items the must-haves for a smooth and enjoyable road trip.

Comfort Essentials

a. Clothing and Layers

France's weather varies widely depending on the season and region. From the chilly Alps to the balmy Riviera, packing versatile clothing is key.

Light layer: include breathable top lightweight sweaters and comfortable pants for unpredictable weather.

Warm Layers: A fleece or insulated jacket is crucial for mountain regions like the French Alps or during winter.

Rain Gear: A compact raincoat or travel umbrella is a lifesaver for sudden downpours, especially in regions like Brittany.

Comfortable Shoes: Bring walking shoes for city strolls and sturdy hiking boots for outdoor adventures.

b. Travel Comfort Items

Neck Pillow and Blanket: Essential for long drives or naps during rest breaks.

Reusable Water Bottles: Staying hydrated is critical, and refillable bottles are eco-friendly and economical.

Snacks: Pack non-perishable options like nuts, granola bars, or dried fruits for hunger pangs between meals.

Entertainment: Audiobooks, music playlists, or podcasts tailored to your tastes can make hours on the road fly by.

c. Personal Care

Toiletry Bag: Include travel-sized versions of toothpaste, shampoo, hand sanitizer, and deodorant.

First Aid Kit: Ensure it contains essential supplies like bandages, antiseptic wipes, pain relievers, and any personal medications you may require.

Tissues and Wet Wipes: These come in handy for quick clean-ups, especially at roadside rest areas.

Safety Essentials

a. Car Safety Equipment

French law mandates that every vehicle carries specific safety items. Ensure your rental or personal vehicle includes:

High-Visibility Vest: Required for every passenger, to be worn in case of a roadside emergency.

Warning Triangle: Used to signal other drivers if your car breaks down.

Headlamp Beam Adjusters: Necessary for vehicles with lights designed for driving on the left side of the road.

Spare Bulbs and Fuses: In case headlights or taillights fail.

Breathalyzer Test Kit: A unique requirement in France, though the enforcement is lenient.

b. Navigation Tools

GPS Device or Smartphone App: Ensure it's updated with the latest maps for French roads. Apps like Waze or ViaMichelin are particularly useful for real-time updates on traffic and speed cameras.

Paper Map: A physical map is invaluable in rural areas where cellular signals may be weak.

c. Emergency Numbers and Documentation

Roadside Assistance Numbers: Save the number for your car Rental Company or insurance provider.

International Driving Permit (IDP): If required, ensure it's valid and packed alongside your regular driver's license.

Vehicle Documents: Include the car's registration papers and proof of insurance.

Convenience Essentials

a. Electronics and Charging

Universal Adapter: In France, Type C and Type E plugs are utilized. A multi-port adapter is ideal for simultaneously charging multiple devices.

Car Charger: Invest in a high-speed USB car charger for phones and GPS devices.

Power Bank: A portable charger ensures your devices stay powered during long stretches without access to outlets.

b. Storage Solutions

Packing Cubes: These help organize clothing and save space in your luggage.

Roof Box or Trunk Organizer: Ideal for keeping gear, groceries, or suitcases neatly arranged.

Packing Tips for Efficiency

Create a Checklist: Write down everything you'll need and check items off as you pack.

Pack Light: Stick to essentials and avoid overpacking. Remember, you can always do laundry or purchase items en route.

Keep Essentials Accessible: Store critical items like travel documents, snacks, and a first aid kit in easily reachable spots.

Packing thoughtfully ensures a hassle-free and enjoyable road trip across France. By including comfort items, safety equipment, and convenient tools, you're prepared for any scenario

Best Practices for a Stress-Free Journey

Embarking on a road trip across France can be an exciting adventure, but traveling with kids or pets adds a layer of complexity that requires careful planning. Whether you're navigating winding mountain roads, exploring charming villages, or cruising along coastal highways, ensuring the comfort and well-being of your young passengers or furry companions is essential. This comprehensive guide will help you have a stress-free and enjoyable trip.

Traveling with Kids

Children bring a sense of wonder to any trip, but they also require attention, entertainment, and patience. Here's a comprehensive guide to making sure your journey is enjoyable and stress-free.

a. Pre-Trip Preparation

Involve Them in Planning

Allow older kids to help choose destinations or activities. Feeling involved makes them more excited about the trip.

Show them pictures or videos of landmarks they'll visit to build anticipation.

Pack Strategically

Comfort Items: Bring favorite blankets, stuffed animals, or pillows to create a cozy environment in the car.

Snacks and Drinks: Pack a variety of healthy, mess-free snacks like fruit slices, granola bars, or crackers. Avoid sugary treats that can cause hyperactivity.

Clothing: Include layers for unpredictable weather and comfortable outfits for long rides.

Schedule Breaks

To give youngsters a chance to stretch and burn off some energy, plan stops at parks, rest areas, or attractions every two to three hours.

b. Entertainment on the Road

Screen-Free Activities

Bring travel-friendly games like magnetic chess, card decks, or coloring books.

Create a scavenger hunt with items to spot along the road (e.g., cows, castles, or specific road signs).

Tech Solutions

Load tablets with kid-friendly apps, movies, or audiobooks. Noise-canceling headphones ensure a peaceful ride for everyone.

c. Car Safety for Kids

Child Seats

Ensure you have an appropriate car seat or booster seat that complies with French regulations.

Double-check that the seat is properly installed before starting your journey.

Seatbelt Checks

Reinforce the importance of keeping seatbelts fastened throughout the trip.

Traveling with Pets

Pets are beloved companions, and France is notably pet-friendly, with many accommodations and restaurants welcoming them. Nonetheless, a road trip with pets demands additional care for their needs and comfort.

a. Pre-Trip Preparation

Visit the Vet

To ensure that your pet is healthy enough to travel, schedule a visit with the veterinarian.

Update vaccinations and ask about calming remedies if your pet is anxious.

Documentation

Bring your pet's vaccination records, especially for international travel.

Personalize an ID tag or microchip with your contact information.

b. Packing Essentials for Pets

Food and Water: Pack enough food for the trip, along with collapsible bowls.

Leash and Collar: Keep a sturdy leash and harness for walks at rest stops or attractions.

Bed or Blanket: Bring a familiar item to help your pet feel secure in unfamiliar environments.

Cleaning Supplies: Include poop bags, litter (for cats), and cleaning wipes for accidents.

c. Comfort and Safety in the Car

Secure Travel

Position the crate in a well-ventilated space, sheltered from direct sunlight.

Regular Breaks

Take breaks every two to three hours so your pet can relieve itself, drink water, and stretch its legs.

d. Managing Stress

Comforting Techniques

Play calming music or use pet-friendly soothing sprays.

Avoid feeding your pet just before the trip to reduce the risk of motion sickness.

Desensitization

If your pet isn't used to long car rides, take short practice drives leading up to the trip.

Kid-and-Pet-Friendly Destinations in France

For Kids

Disneyland Paris: An enchanting adventure for children of every age.

Cité des Sciences et de l'Industrie (Paris): Hands-on exhibits and activities to engage curious minds.

Beaches in Brittany: Sandy shores with shallow waters ideal for family playtime.

For Pets

French Riviera Beaches: Many coastal spots are dog-friendly, especially in off-peak seasons.

Alsace Villages: Quiet streets and scenic trails perfect for leashed walks.

General Tips for a Harmonious Journey

Prepare for Emergencies

Save local veterinary numbers and emergency services on your phone.

Put together a first aid kit tailored for pets or children, including essentials such as antiseptic, bandages, and medications.

Monitor both kids and pets for signs of fatigue or overstimulation. Adjust your itinerary as needed.

Stay Flexible

Accept that delays or unexpected detours may happen. Maintaining a relaxed attitude helps everyone stay at ease.

Traveling with kids or pets requires thoughtful planning, but the joy they bring to the journey makes the effort worthwhile. With the right preparation and a focus on comfort and safety, your road trip through France can become a cherished memory for all members of the family human and furry alike.

Verdon Gorge

régional
du Verdon

D952

La Palud-sur-Verdon

BOULOGNE

Point de vue

D952

SCAN HERE

HOW TO USE QR CODE

- Open your phone's camera app or download scanner app from play store or apple store
- Point the camera at the QR code for a few seconds (no need to take a photo).
- A link should appear on the display, leading you to the location of the code

Loire Valley

SCAN HERE

HOW TO USE QR CODE

- Open your phone's camera app or download scanner app from play store or apple store
- Point the camera at the QR code for a few seconds (no need to take a photo).
- A link should appear on the display, leading you to the location of the code

Dordogne

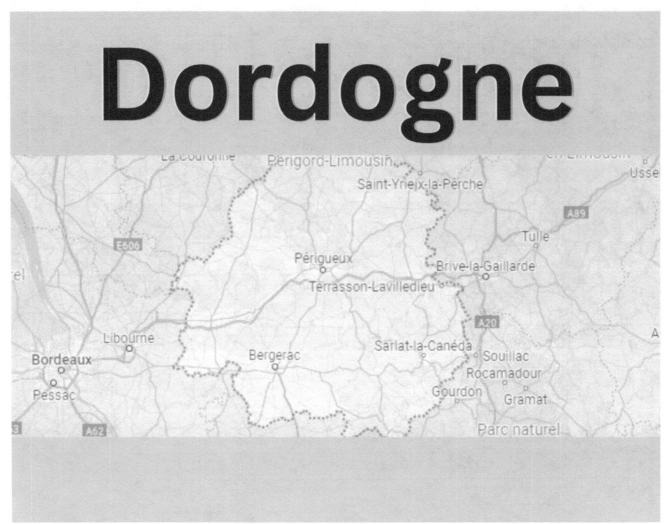

SCAN HERE

HOW TO USE QR CODE

- Open your phone's camera app or download scanner app from play store or apple store
- Point the camera at the QR code for a few seconds (no need to take a photo).
- A link should appear on the display, leading you to the location of the code

Provence

SCAN HERE

HOW TO USE QR CODE

- Open your phone's camera app or download scanner app from play store or apple store
- Point the camera at the QR code for a few seconds (no need to take a photo).
- A link should appear on the display, leading you to the location of the code

Sarlat-la-Canéda

SCAN HERE

HOW TO USE QR CODE

- Open your phone's camera app or download scanner app from play store or apple store
- Point the camera at the QR code for a few seconds (no need to take a photo).
- A link should appear on the display, leading you to the location of the code

French Riviera

SCAN HERE

HOW TO USE QR CODE

- Open your phone's camera app or download scanner app from play store or apple store
- Point the camera at the QR code for a few seconds (no need to take a photo).
- A link should appear on the display, leading you to the location of the code

B&B HOTEL Paris Porte des Lilas

SCAN HERE

HOW TO USE QR CODE

- Open your phone's camera app or download scanner app from play store or apple store
- Point the camera at the QR code for a few seconds (no need to take a photo).
- A link should appear on the display, leading you to the location of the code

Bordeaux

SCAN HERE

HOW TO USE QR CODE

- Open your phone's camera app or download scanner app from play store or apple store
- Point the camera at the QR code for a few seconds (no need to take a photo).
- A link should appear on the display, leading you to the location of the code

Carrefour supermarket

SCAN HERE   HOW TO USE QR CODE

- Open your phone's camera app or download scanner app from play store or apple store
- Point the camera at the QR code for a few seconds (no need to take a photo).
- A link should appear on the display, leading you to the location of the code

Disneyland Paris

Vapiano Disney
Village Pasta Pizza Bar
Italian

Disneyland Paris

SCAN HERE

HOW TO USE QR CODE

- Open your phone's camera app or download scanner app from play store or apple store
- Point the camera at the QR code for a few seconds (no need to take a photo).
- A link should appear on the display, leading you to the location of the code

Chapter 9

FAQs about Driving in France from Parking Rules to Fuel Options

Navigating the roads of France often prompts questions, particularly for travelers unfamiliar with the country's driving laws, fuel systems, and parking norms. Here's a detailed breakdown of common inquiries and their solutions to ensure your trip is smooth and stress-free.

1. What Are the Parking Rules in France?

a. Types of Parking Zones

Blue Zones (Zone Bleue):

These areas, found in many towns and cities, allow free parking for a limited time (usually 1–2 hours).To indicate your arrival time, you must display a parking disc, available at local shops or tourist offices.

Paid Parking Zones (Zones Payantes)

Marked by street signs and parking meters. Payment is required during specific hours, often from 9:00 AM to 7:00 PM, excluding Sundays and holidays.

Underground Parking (Parking Souterrain)

Common in urban centers, these secure facilities are ideal for long-term parking.

b. Prohibited Parking

Refrain from parking in zones designated by yellow or white zigzag lines. Double parking or blocking traffic is not allowed and may lead to fines or towing.

c. Apps for Parking Assistance

Use apps like Parkopedia or PayByPhone to locate and pay for parking.

2. What Are the Fuel Options in France?

a. Fuel Types

Diesel (Gazole): Widely available and commonly used for many vehicles in France.

Unleaded Petrol (Sans Plomb 95, Sans Plomb 98): Standard fuel for most cars.

E85 (Superethanol): This biofuel is cheaper and available at select stations. It is only suitable for compatible vehicles.

Electric Charging (Recharge Électrique): EV stations are becoming increasingly accessible, especially along major routes and in urban areas.

b. Finding Fuel Stations

Utilize applications such as Waze, Google Maps, or Chargemap to help electric vehicle users find nearby charging stations.

Stations along autoroutes often have higher fuel prices than those in towns.

c. Payment Options

Most stations accept credit cards, though some rural locations may only take cash.

Automated fuel pumps require a chip-and-PIN card.

3. Is an International Driving Permit (IDP) needed to drive in France?

For EU/EEA license holders: An IDP is not necessary; your license is recognized throughout France.

Non-EU License Holders

Travelers from countries like the USA, Canada, or Australia may need an IDP in addition to their home license.

Examine the particular validity requirements associated with your country of origin.

4. What Should I Do If I Get Pulled Over by Police?

Documentation to Provide

Driver's license, vehicle registration (carte grise), and insurance papers (green card).

IDP, if applicable.

Key Tips

Stay polite and remain in your vehicle unless asked to step out.

If issued a fine, it must be paid immediately for non-residents.

5. How Do I Handle Roadside Emergencies?

a. Emergency Numbers

Dial 112 for all emergencies.

Roadside assistance services, such as AXA Assistance or Mondial Assistance, can be contacted for vehicle issues.

b. Required Equipment in Your Car

Reflective vests for all passengers.

Warning triangle to place on the road in case of a breakdown.

Breathalyzer kits (although no longer mandatory, carrying one is recommended).

6. Are There Restrictions on Driving in Cities?

Yes, many cities have low-emission zones (Zones à Faibles Émissions, ZFE) to reduce pollution.

Crit'Air Stickers:

Required to enter these zones. Stickers must be applied to your windshield and indicate your vehicle's emissions level.

Obtain them online through the official government portal.

Times of Enforcement

Restrictions often apply during peak pollution periods, with fines for non-compliance.

7. What Are the Typical Traffic Violations and Their Penalties?

a. Speeding Fines vary from €68 to €1,500 based on the level of the offense.

Speed limits:

Urban areas: 50 km/h

Open roads: 80–90 km/h

Autoroutes: 130 km/h (or 110 km/h in rain).

b. Phone Usage

Hands-free devices are allowed, but holding a phone while driving incurs a fine of €135.

c. Alcohol Limits

Standard limit: 0.05% blood alcohol content (BAC).

For new drivers: 0.02% BAC.

8. Can I Use Public Rest Stops (Aires) for Overnight Stays?

Yes, rest stops often allow brief overnight stays, particularly for campervans.

Facilities range from basic parking to fully equipped areas with showers, picnic spots, and playgrounds.

9. Is Car Insurance Mandatory in France?

Yes, all vehicles must have third-party liability insurance at a minimum.

International travelers should check if their home policy covers them in France or purchase additional coverage.

Driving in France can be a gratifying experience, but it comes with its unique regulations and customs. By understanding parking regulations, fuel systems, and common road practices, you'll be better equipped to navigate the country's diverse landscapes confidently.

How to Handle Breakdowns Accidents or Getting Lost

Even with careful preparation, unforeseen difficulties can occur during any road trip. From vehicle breakdowns to navigating unfamiliar roads, knowing how to handle these situations can make the difference between a minor hiccup and a trip-derailing event. Here's a comprehensive guide to managing common road trip issues in France.

1. Vehicle Breakdowns

Breakdowns are among the most frequent problems encountered by travelers during road trips. Fortunately, France has a well-organized system for roadside assistance.

Steps to Take if Your Vehicle Breaks Down

Ensure Safety First

Move your vehicle to the edge of the road as much as you can. Wear a reflective vest before exiting the vehicle (this is mandatory in France).

Place the warning triangle at least 30 meters (about 100 feet) behind your car to warn of approaching traffic.

Contact Roadside Assistance

Call 112 for emergencies or 17 for police help.

Use a dedicated roadside assistance service such as:

Autoroutes Assistance: Dial 0800 00 60 00 for help on toll roads.

Private Breakdown Services: AXA Assistance, Europ Assistance, or Mondial Assistance offer support for travelers.

On autoroutes, walk to the nearest orange emergency phone for direct assistance. Towing services on highways must be arranged by the autoroute operator, and private towing is prohibited.

Know Your Insurance Policy

Many car rental companies or travel insurance policies include roadside assistance. Keep the contact number and policy details handy.

Plan for Repairs or Temporary Transport

Larger towns and cities will have repair shops, known as garages. If immediate repair isn't possible, consider renting a car for the interim.

2. Road Accidents

In the unfortunate event of an accident, staying calm and following the proper procedures is crucial.

Steps to Handle an Accident

Check for Injuries

Make sure the safety of all passengers and anyone else involved is prioritized. Contact 112 for any medical emergencies.

Secure the Scene

Activate the hazard lights and set up the reflective triangle.

Avoid moving vehicles unless it's necessary for safety.

Exchange Information

Gather details from all parties involved:

Full names, addresses, and contact numbers.

License plate numbers and vehicle make/models.

Insurance information, including policy numbers.

Fill Out a Constat Amiable (Accident Report)

This standardized form is used in France to document accidents. If available, fill it out with the other driver to speed up insurance claims. Copies can be obtained from your insurance provider or car Rental Company.

Involve Authorities if Necessary

If there are injuries, significant damage, or disputes, contacts the police (17) to file a formal report.

Notify Your Insurance Provider

Report the incident promptly to your car rental agency or personal insurer.

3. Getting Lost

Getting lost can be a frustrating but often manageable experience, especially with today's technology.

Preventative Measures

Download Maps Offline:

Apps like Google Maps, Maps. Me or Waze allows you to download routes in advance for offline use.

Carry a Paper Map

In rural areas with poor network coverage, having a traditional map can be invaluable.

Steps to Take If You Get Lost

Stop and Reassess

Find a secure place to pull over. Attempting to find your way while driving raises the chances of accidents.

Seek Local Help

Don't hesitate to request directions from locals. Many people in France are willing to assist, and a courteous demeanor can make a big difference. Get acquainted with helpful expressions like:

"Pouvez-vous m'aider ?" (Can you help me?)

"Où se trouve... ?" (Where is...?)

Use Apps for Assistance

Apps like GeoGuessr or What3Words can help pinpoint your exact location.

Identify Landmarks

Look for distinct landmarks, road signs, or names of nearby towns to help reorient yourself.

Consider Re-Routing:

If you're significantly off-course, returning to a main road or following signs to a larger town or city can help you regain your bearings.

4. Language Barriers

Although many French people speak English, especially in tourist-heavy areas, language barriers can still pose a challenge in rural regions.

Solutions

Translation Apps: Use tools like Google Translate for real-time assistance.

Prepare Key Phrases: Learn basic French words and phrases for emergencies or directions.

Printed Resources: Carry a phrasebook with essential vocabulary for driving and roadside situations.

Unexpected challenges on a road trip in France are manageable with the right knowledge and preparation. Whether it's a breakdown, an accident, or losing your way, the key is to stay calm and follow these outlined steps. With proper resources at hand and a flexible mindset, you'll be back on track and enjoying the journey in no time.

Important Resources for Travelers Contact Numbers and Websites

Having reliable resources at your fingertips can make your journey across France smooth and stress-free. Whether you're seeking roadside assistance, emergency help, or travel inspiration, these contacts and websites provide essential support for travelers.

1. Emergency Services

France has a well-organized system for handling emergencies, and knowing the right numbers is crucial.

Key Emergency Numbers in France

112: General European emergency number (police, ambulance, fire brigade).

15: Medical emergencies.

17: Police assistance.

18: Fire brigade.

114: SMS-based emergency assistance (for hearing- or speech-impaired individuals).

How to Use Emergency Services Effectively

Clearly state your location, the nature of the emergency, and whether there are injuries.

If you're unsure which number to call, dial 112, which connect to a multilingual operator.

2. Roadside Assistance

Breakdowns or car troubles are common concerns during road trips. These services ensure prompt assistance.

Autoroute Emergency Contacts

Use orange emergency phones along the autoroutes for direct contact with local roadside services.

Autoroutes Assistance: Dial 0800 00 60 00 for issues on toll roads.

Private Roadside Assistance Services:

AXA Assistance: Comprehensive travel and roadside assistance for insured drivers.

Europ Assistance: Offers vehicle recovery, towing, and breakdown services.

Club Identicar: Specialized services for tourists driving in France.

Rental Car Assistance

Check your rental car agreement for roadside assistance coverage. Most companies like Hertz, Europcar, and Avis offer 24/7 support.

3. Driving and Navigation Resources

Keeping updated with driving regulations and traffic conditions is vital.

Websites for Traffic and Route Planning

Bison Futé (www.bison-fute.gouv.fr): Provides live traffic updates, roadworks information, and weather conditions for French roads.

Viamichelin (www.viamichelin.com): Detailed route planning, including toll calculations and travel times.

Waze (www.waze.com): Real-time traffic updates and alternative route suggestions.

Driving Law Updates

Government Portal (www.service-public.fr): Official updates on driving laws, environmental zones, and Crit'Air sticker requirements.

Crit'Air Certification (www.certificat-air.gouv.fr): Information on obtaining the Crit'Air emissions sticker.

4. Accommodation and Dining

Finding quality lodging and local cuisine is essential for a fulfilling trip.

Booking Platforms

Gîtes de France (www.gites-de-france.com): Authentic guesthouses and rural accommodations.

Camping France (www.campingfrance.com): Find campsites and caravan parks across the country.

Booking.com and Airbnb: Wide range of hotels, guesthouses, and unique stays.

Dining Guides:

La Fourchette (www.lafourchette.com): Restaurant recommendations and bookings.

Michelin Guide (guide.michelin.com): Listings of starred restaurants and local dining gems.

5. Tourism and Cultural Resources

France's diverse regions offer unique experiences, and these resources help you make the most of your visit.

Regional Tourism Websites

Paris (www.parisinfo.com): Official tourism site for Paris and Île-de-France.

Provence-Alpes-Côte d'Azur (www.provence-alpes-cotedazur.com): Explore Provence's landscapes, culture, and cuisine.

Loire Valley (www.loirevalley-france.co.uk): Guides to châteaux, wine tours, and regional events.

National Tourism:

France.fr (www.france.fr): The official French tourism website with insights into attractions, itineraries, and events.

6. Language Assistance

Language barriers can be a challenge, but these tools simplify communication.

Translation Apps

Google Translate: Offline language packs are especially useful for rural areas.

DeepL Translator: Known for accuracy in nuanced translations.

Phrasebooks and Guides

Carry a compact French phrasebook for emergencies or local interactions.

7. Fuel and EV Charging Stations

Staying fueled up—whether for traditional or electric vehicles—is crucial for uninterrupted travel.

Fuel Station Locators

TotalEnergies (www.totalenergies.fr): Find fuel stations with amenities like food, restrooms, and Wi-Fi.

Esso France (www.esso.fr): Nationwide network of reliable fuel stations.

EV Charging Networks

Chargemap (www.chargemap.com): Locate EV charging points and plan EV-friendly routes.

PlugShare (www.plugshare.com): Community-sourced reviews of charging stations.

8. Healthcare Resources

Travelers occasionally need medical attention while abroad.

Finding Hospitals and Clinics

Use Doctolib (www.doctolib.fr) to book medical appointments online.

Pharmacies are widely available and marked with a green cross; many offer basic medical advice.

Health Insurance Assistance

Contact your travel insurance provider for details on covered healthcare services.

9. Apps and Digital Tools

Technology is your best friend on the road. These apps can simplify every aspect of your trip.

Google Maps/Waze: Reliable navigation and traffic monitoring.

PackPoint: Helps plan your packing list based on destination and weather.

XE Currency: Quick currency conversions to manage expenses.

TripIt: Organize travel itineraries in one place.

10. Cultural and Historical Insights

Enrich your journey with knowledge about France's heritage.

Museums of France (www.musees-france.fr): Information on exhibits, opening hours, and ticketing for major museums.

UNESCO Sites in France (www.unesco.org/france): Explore a full list of UNESCO World Heritage Sites in the country.

11. Additional Traveler Support

For any situation not covered above, these general resources can be helpful:

Embassies and Consulates: Check your country's embassy website in France for assistance.

Rail Information (www.sncf.com): While focused on trains, SNCF also provides combined road-and-rail travel advice.

Equipping yourself with these essential resources ensures a smoother, more enjoyable road trip across France. From planning your routes to handling emergencies, these tools, contacts, and websites are your safety net for an unforgettable journey.

Chapter 10

Why France is the Ultimate Road Trip Destination

France, a land of unparalleled beauty, history, and cultural wealth, is the quintessential road trip destination. From the snow-covered summits of the French Alps to the sun-drenched shores of the Côte d'Azur, each bend in the road presents a touch of enchantment. As you navigate its varied landscapes, you'll encounter breathtaking coastal views, verdant vineyards, medieval towns frozen in time, and bustling cities brimming with life. Few countries can rival the diverse experiences France offers, making it an irresistible choice for adventurers and dreamers alike.

A Tapestry of Landscapes

France's geography is as diverse as its people. Picture this: one day, you're driving along the winding roads of the Loire Valley, with its majestic châteaux rising from the mist. The next, you're cruising the Route des Grandes Alpes, where towering mountain peaks and crystalline lakes take your breath away. The vast lavender fields of Provence, the rugged cliffs of Normandy, and the tranquil countryside of Burgundy all create a unique patchwork of scenic beauty.

Each region tells a story, not just in its landscapes but also in its architecture, traditions, and cuisine. France is more than a destination it's an ever-changing journey, where every mile brings something new and unforgettable.

A Journey through Time

Traveling through France is like stepping into the pages of history. Imagine standing where Joan of Arc rallied her troops or walking the same cobbled streets that Napoleon once trod. The castles, fortresses, and historical landmarks scattered across the country are not mere relics but vivid reminders of France's profound influence on world history.

Road trippers have the unique opportunity to connect these historical dots, moving seamlessly from Roman amphitheaters in Nîmes to the hallowed beaches of Normandy, from the medieval charm of Carcassonne to the grand opulence of Versailles. With France, history isn't just something you learn about—it's something you live.

Culture at Every Corner

France's cultural diversity is one of its most important assets. Trips allow you to immerse yourself in local life in a way no other travel method can. Stroll through bustling farmers' markets brimming with fresh produce and artisanal goods. Visit quiet artisan workshops where traditions have been passed down for generations. And don't miss the opportunity to join local festivals that light up small towns and cities alike, offering an authentic glimpse into French joie de vivre.

Each stop introduces you to new traditions, dialects, and specialties—from Burgundy's fine wines to Brittany's buttery crêpes. Whether you're an art lover, a foodie, or someone who simply loves meeting new people, France has something to ignite your passions.

 The first step toward creating your road trip story. Let this book be your trusted companion as you venture through the landscapes and layers of France. Think about the thrill of your first glimpse of the Eiffel Tower, the serenity of a sunset over Provence's lavender fields, or the pride in navigating a scenic drive that leads to an unforgettable hidden village.

France is ready to reveal itself to you, one road, one-stop, and one moment at a time. So fuel your wanderlust, start marking your map, and let the journey begin. Your ultimate adventure awaits grabs your keys and discover France like never before.

Call to Action: Share Your French Adventure

Now that you're equipped with all the knowledge, tips, and inspiration needed to embark on your ultimate French road trip, it's time to hit the road and make memories of your own. Whether you're traversing the wine routes of Burgundy, marveling at the cliffs of Normandy, or savoring local delicacies in a quaint Provençal village, each journey will be uniquely yours.

Start Your Journey

France is waiting for you with open roads and endless possibilities. Take the plunge—begin planning, pack your essentials, and set off on an adventure that promises to enrich your life with new sights, flavors, and experiences. Every road leads to a story, and every turn reveals something new.

Use this guide as your trusted travel companion. Highlight your chosen routes, jot down must-visit spots, and keep it close as you navigate the highways and byways of this captivating country. Keep in mind that the journey holds as much significance as the destination.

Share Your Experiences

We'd love to hear about your adventures! Every traveler sees France through a unique lens, and your stories add to the rich tapestry of road trip memories. Did you discover a hidden treasure away from the usual tourist routes? Did a spontaneous detour lead to an unforgettable experience? Whether it's photos of stunning vistas, reviews of cozy guesthouses, or tales of serendipitous encounters, your journey could inspire others to create their own.

Consider sharing your road trip tales on social media or travel platforms. Use hashtags like #RoadTripFrance or #DiscoverFrance2025 to join a community of explorers who, like you, have been captivated by this incredible country.

Continue Exploring

Let this be the first of many road trips through France. With its rich history, varied geography, and endless cultural treasures, there's always more to discover. Perhaps your next trip will take you deeper into the Alps, further into the heart of the Dordogne Valley, or to the sunny coasts of Corsica. Keep this guide handy for future explorations—it's a resource designed to grow with your adventures.

Make It Yours

The beauty of road travel lies in its spontaneity and freedom. So, while this guide provides a framework, don't be afraid to forge your path. Create an itinerary that reflects your passions, indulge in unplanned stops, and embrace the unexpected moments that make travel so rewarding.

Now is the time to fuel your wanderlust, embrace your adventurous spirit, and set forth on a journey through one of the most beautiful countries in the world. France awaits—go and experience it for yourself.

Made in United States
Cleveland, OH
12 July 2025

Made in the USA
Columbia, SC
31 May 2025

58731816R00054